BRAIN

INNER WORKINGS OF THE
GREY MATTER

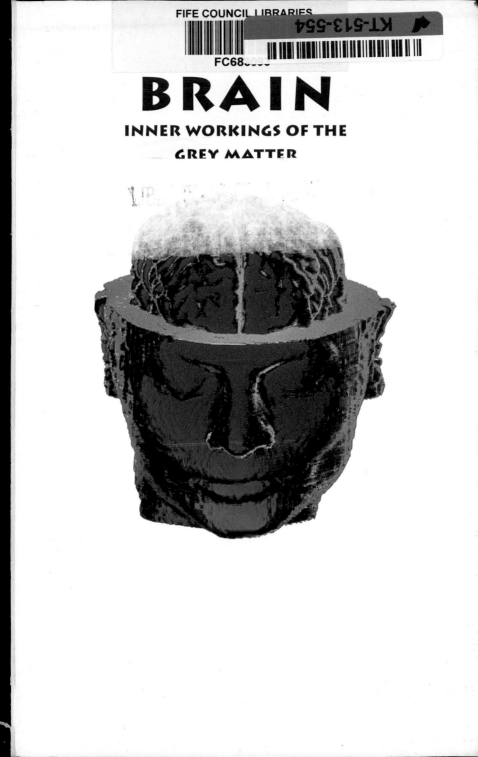

BRAIN
INNER WORKINGS OF THE
GREY MATTER

By
Richard Walker

Consultant
Dr Gabrielle Murphy

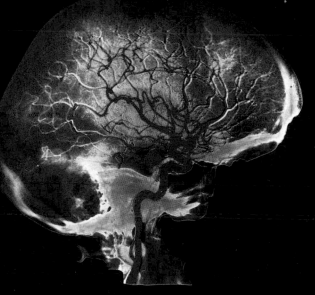

A Dorling Kindersley Book

Dorling **DK** Kindersley

LONDON, NEW YORK, MUNICH,
MELBOURNE, and DELHI

Project Editor Steve Setford
Project Art Editor Peter Radcliffe
Senior Editor Fran Jones
Senior Art Editor Stefan Podhorodecki
Category Publisher Jayne Parsons
Managing Art Editor Jacquie Gulliver
Picture Researcher Brenda Clynch
DK Picture Library Sally Hamilton,
Sarah Mills, Rose Horridge
Production Erica Rosen
DTP Designer Siu Yin Ho

First published in Great Britain in 2002 by
Dorling Kindersley Limited
80 Strand, London WC2R 0RL

2 4 6 8 10 9 7 5 3 1

Copyright © 2002 Dorling Kindersley Limited

The CIP Catalogue record for this book is available
from the British Library

ISBN 0-7513-3750-1

Reproduced by Colourscan, Singapore
Printed and bound by L.E.G.O., Italy

See our complete
catalogue at
www.dk.com

CONTENTS

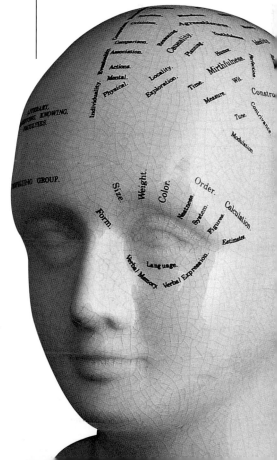

INTRODUCTION

What's cauliflower-sized, wrinkled, pink, and squashy? The answer is… your brain! Although you take it for granted, your brain is quite amazing. It has no memory chips, but it holds as much information as a 20-volume encyclopedia. It moves your body, even though the brain itself has no moving parts. Most importantly, it's what makes you an individual human being.

Humans aren't the only creatures with brains – most other animals have them too. A brain is the control centre of an animal's body. It keeps a check on what's happening in the animal's surroundings, figures out what's going on, and then

THE BRAIN COMMUNICATES WITH THE REST OF THE BODY THROUGH NERVES, SHOWN HERE.

tells the body what to do.
Your own brain does all
these things, as well
as enabling
you to

think, learn, love, imagine,
remember, and everything
else that makes you the person you are today.

A SHARK'S BRAIN HELPS IT TO TRACK DOWN PREY IN THE OCEAN.

Of course, brains don't exist on their own. Read on, and you'll see how a network of nerves relays information to and from the brain at lightning speed. You'll also find out how your skin, nose, tongue, ears, and eyes send messages along these nerves so that the brain can make you feel, hear, smell, taste, and see. Discover how, incredibly, some animals' senses work in different ways to ours, so they can detect electricity or even "see" heat. By the end of the book you'll understand why we humans, and other animals, behave the way we do – whether we're playing, communicating, getting angry, or just being kind to each other. But whatever the behaviour, the brain is always in control.

For those of you who want to explore the subject in more detail, there are Log On "bites" that appear throughout the book. These will direct you to some fascinating websites, where you can check out even more about the brain.

So turn the pages, and prepare to have your mind boggled by your own brain!

Richard Walker.

BRAIN STORY

I t's official! Of all the animals in the world, humans are the smartest. This is down to the squidgy stuff between our ears – our brains. We use them to think, imagine, remember, and so much more besides. Other animals may not be as clever as us, but they still use their brains to find food and mates, avoid danger, and generally survive. But why and how did animals develop brains in the first place?

Beginnings of the brain

The story of the brain starts way back in time – some 600 million years ago, in fact – with the first animals that appeared in the Earth's oceans. Many of these creatures could not move about but clung tightly to rocks and other solid objects. Here they sat, quite content, waiting for food to float past. When it did, they grabbed it with their tentacles and wolfed it down, just as sea anemones, their descendants, do today.

Nerve networks

The bodies of these creatures, like those of all living things (including you), were made up of microscopic building blocks called cells. Some of these cells, called nerve cells, were linked together to form a network that carried messages around the body

A SEA ANEMONE DOESN'T HAVE A BRAIN, BUT IT DOES POSSESS A SIMPLE NERVE NETWORK.

A CLOSE-UP VIEW OF A FLY'S HEAD REVEALS AN ARRAY OF SENSORS, INCLUDING LARGE EYES (GREEN) AND A PAIR OF STUBBY ANTENNAE THAT ARE SENSITIVE TO VIBRATIONS AND SMELLS.

at high speed. When a piece of food touched the animal's body, this "nerve net" sent a command telling the muscles to pull the tentacles in towards the mouth. The nerve net was effective, but it was too simple to be called a brain.

On the move

From those early animals that spent their lives stuck fast to the rocks, there evolved more adventurous creatures who were determined

ANTENNA

FORGET BACTERIA, FUNGI, AND PLANTS...THEY'RE BRAINLESS

to move around and explore their neighbourhood. An animal that can actively move from place to place generally moves in only one direction (forwards), so it has a front end and a back end. The front end – or anterior end, as zoologists (animal scientists) like to call it – is the first part of an animal that encounters its surroundings.

Over time, some of the nerve cells at the front end of mobile animals developed into sensors that responded to touch, light, chemicals, and so on. This meant that the animals didn't bump into rocks and could detect their next meal. (Get down on all fours, start moving backwards, and you'll soon see how useful these sensors are!)

9

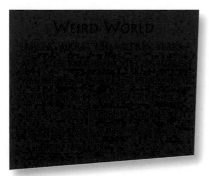

The cerebral ganglia sorted out all the information coming from the sensors and then sent instructions to the rest of the body, such as "Swim away from the large, hungry predator that's just about to eat me!" or "Hurry up and catch that juicy worm!" At the same time, an identifiable bit at the front end of the body, better known as the head, came into being. The head contained the brain, and – depending on the type of animal – bristled with eyes, ears, antennae, and other sensors (oh, and a mouth to let food in, but that's another story!).

Simple brains

As these sensors appeared at the front of the body, so too did special clusters of nerve cells. Scientists call these clusters cerebral ganglia, but we can think of them as simple brains.

Think about any animals living today, from ants and bats to fleas and crayfish, and you'll find that they all have the same basic arrangement.

Expanding brains

The earliest prototypes of what would become the human brain can be seen in fish, the most ancient of the vertebrates (animals with backbones). The nerve cells in a fish's head are organized into a brain with three sections – a hindbrain in

WEIRD WORLD

charge of balance and hearing, a midbrain dealing with vision, and a forebrain that controls the sense of smell. This type of brain structure evolved with the first vertebrates 500 million years ago. It can still be found today in fish, reptiles, and amphibians.

In more advanced vertebrates, such as birds and mammals, the different parts of the brain have expanded to take on other roles. The forebrain has grown to co-ordinate the senses, provide memory, and allow learning. In mammals it has developed into the cerebrum – the "thinking" part of the brain. A region of the hindbrain, the cerebellum, has also expanded. It permits birds and mammals to perform more complex feats of balance and movement than reptiles, fish, and amphibians can.

B igger brains

Like cats, dogs, and horses, we humans are mammals. Our closest mammal relatives are chimpanzees, so it shouldn't come as a surprise to hear that we're descended from ape-like ancestors. Of all the changes that occurred during human evolution, two really stand out.

THE LARGE CEREBELLUM AT THE BACK OF A CAT'S BRAIN GIVES IT FANTASTIC BALANCE WHEN CLIMBING. IT ALSO GIVES THE CAT THE ABILITY TO RIGHT ITSELF IF IT FALLS FROM A HEIGHT, AS SHOWN HERE.

The first was the switch from walking on all fours to standing on two feet. The second was the rapid growth in brain size. A great leap forward came with the appearance of our ancient relative *Homo erectus* ("upright man") over 2 million years ago. *Homo erectus*'s brain had expanded to a size halfway between a chimpanzee's and a modern human's. This might not seem very big, but it was a great improvement on the previous ancestor's brain. This increase in brain size was mainly due to the expansion of the cerebrum (remember, this is the "thinking" part of the brain).

Being smarter enabled *Homo erectus* to do all sorts of new things, such as making tools and using fire. But by 100,000 years ago, *Homo erectus* had finally become extinct. The stage was set for a bigger-brained relative called *Homo sapiens* (better known as modern humans) to emerge on the scene.

THE WRINKLY SURFACE OF A HUMAN BRAIN IS REVEALED HERE BY A CT SCANNER, WHICH CAN "SEE THROUGH" A PERSON'S SKULL.

LOG ON...
More on mummies at
www.site-ology.com/egypt/

Feeling brainy

The brain of *Homo sapiens* – our brain – weighs around 1.3 kg (2.9 lb), is as soft as butter, and is pinkish-red in colour. The part that has really increased in size is the front of the cerebrum, from where personality and imagination are governed.

Another unique feature of our brain is a part devoted to language, which enables us to communicate through complex speech. As the cranium (the domed bit of the skull) has increased in size to accommodate the growing brain, so our face has got smaller, compared to the faces of our ape cousins and extinct relatives.

Early ideas

Ancient peoples would have had no doubts about the existence of the brain – heads were always being chopped off or cracked open – but there was some confusion about its role. The ancient Egyptians paid little attention to the brain. They thought that the mind and soul were located in the heart and liver. In fact, when Egyptian embalmers prepared dead bodies for mummification, they just pulled the brain out through the nostrils and threw it away, even though most of the other organs were carefully preserved in jars and sealed in the tomb with the mummy.

Changing views

These Egyptian ideas were accepted by the ancient Greeks (that is, the ancient ancient Greeks) until the 5th century BC, when the philosopher Alcmaeon of Croton suggested that the brain, not the heart, was in charge of sensation. This idea held sway until another philosopher,

THIS COLOURFUL MUMMY CASE HELD THE BODY OF AN ANCIENT EGYPTIAN, BUT NOT THE BRAIN. THIS WASN'T THOUGHT TO BE OF ANY USE TO THE DEAD PERSON IN THE AFTERLIFE.

THIS OLD SKULL CLEARLY SHOWS THE HOLE
THAT WAS CUT IN THE BONE TO EXPOSE
THE BRAIN DURING TREPANNING.

served to cool the blood. Fortunately, by the 3rd century BC, Herophilus of Alexandria put things back on track by insisting that the brain was in control of thinking.

Hole in the head

Whatever the experts and scholars were saying, the ordinary people of the ancient world seemed to have no doubt about the link between the brain and thought. For a start, it wasn't unknown for warriors to eat the brains of enemies defeated on the battlefield in order to gain their cunning and wisdom.

In addition, the use of trepanning was widespread. The process of trepanning involved making a hole in the skull to relieve severe headaches called migraines, or to release "evil spirits" that were believed to cause mental illness. A hole was cut through the skin of the scalp using a stone scraper or a knife (remember, there were no anaesthetics!). Then a scraper or a simple drill was used to bore through the bone and expose the brain. We know that some

called Aristotle (4th century BC), turned everything upside down by saying that thoughts and emotions were controlled by the heart, and the brain simply

---

WEIRD WORLD

IT LOOKS AS THOUGH EATING
CERTAIN FISH CAN MAKE US MORE
BRAINY. SCIENTISTS HAVE FOUND
THAT OILS FROM FISH SUCH AS
TUNA, MACKEREL, AND SARDINES
HELP THE BRAIN TO DEVELOP
PROPERLY.

people survived this process, because their skulls show that bone eventually grew back over the hole.

Energy consumer

Today's scientists and doctors know a great deal more about the brain, although there are still some mysteries to unravel. One thing we do know is that a large brain like ours demands vast amounts of energy day and night. Despite making up just 2 per cent of the body's mass, the brain consumes 20 per cent of the body's energy, whether we are sleeping or running a marathon. Blood supplies the brain with the glucose and oxygen necessary to provide this energy. Using the energy is the massive network of nerve cells, called neurons, that make up the most complex organ in the animal kingdom – the human brain.

AN ANGIOGRAM IS AN
X-RAY THAT REVEALS BLOOD
VESSELS. THIS ANGIOGRAM
SHOWS THE MAIN ARTERY AND
ITS BRANCHES THAT SUPPLY
THE BRAIN WITH BLOOD.

WHAT A NERVE!

You know what it means to feel nervous, but what exactly is the nervous system, and how is it linked to the brain? The body's nervous system is made up of the brain, the spinal cord, and a network of nerves that relays messages to and from all parts of the body using electrical signals. However, it is only fairly recently that scientists have understood the true nature of nerve cells.

Brain stain

By the middle of the 19th century, scientists had shown that most parts of the human body were made up of cells. They had done this by creating different stains to colour the cells' contents and make them visible under the microscope. But no-one had succeeded in finding a stain that would colour brain cells – assuming, of course, that they actually existed.

Enter Camillo Golgi (1843–1926), an Italian doctor who was fascinated by the structure of the nervous system. In 1872, Golgi was working in a hospital near Milan. Here he set up a laboratory in a tiny kitchen, where he worked during breaks between patients. He tried all sorts of chemicals to stain brain tissue, but none of them worked.

Golgi's big breakthrough came purely by accident. One day he accidentally dropped a slice of brain into a solution of silver nitrate. A few weeks later, he tipped this solution away and out slipped the bit of brain.

CAMILLO GOLGI'S STAIN MADE BRAIN CELLS SHOW UP AS A PATTERN OF BLACK ON GOLD WHEN SEEN UNDER A MICROSCOPE (THE BACKGROUND TO THIS PAGE).

Feeling a little curious, Golgi looked at the brain slice under the microscope. To his delight and astonishment, he noticed lots of black blobs connected by tangles of fibres against a golden background. By an amazing stroke of luck, he had discovered nerve cells, later to be called neurons.

C ommunication network
Golgi's stain, which is still used today, only reveals 10 per cent of the neurons in the brain – which is a good job, because there are something

WEIRD WORLD
THE 12,000 OR SO NEURONS THAT ARE LOST EACH DAY FROM AN ADULT'S BRAIN ARE NOT REPLACED. LUCKILY, THERE ARE BILLIONS OF NEURONS LEFT BEHIND, SO THIS LOSS DOESN'T AFFECT THE WAY THE BRAIN WORKS.

A NEWBORN BABY'S BRAIN HAS A FULL SET OF BRAIN CELLS, BUT IS JUST ONE QUARTER THE SIZE OF AN ADULT'S BRAIN.

like 100 billion (that's 100,000,000,000) brain neurons altogether. If the Golgi stain revealed them all, you'd simply see a mass of black. Each neuron connects with hundreds or even thousands of others. Together, they form a communications network far more complex and sophisticated than any computer.

Although a newborn baby already has his or her full quota of brain neurons, the brain still gets bigger during childhood. The reason? Well, it's because of all the new connections that are made between neurons as the young human experiences the world. In fact, by the time that a baby reaches adulthood,

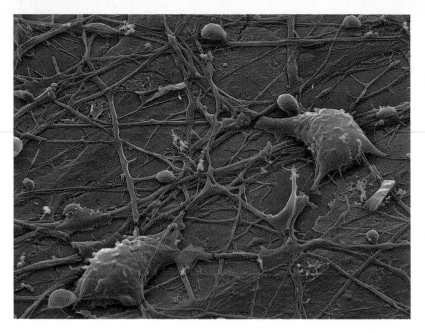

THE TWO BIG BLOBS IN THIS IMAGE ARE BRAIN NEURONS. THE THIN STRANDS ARE DENDRITES – THE BRANCHES THAT RECEIVE IMPULSES FROM NEIGHBOURING NEURONS.

his or her brain will have increased in size four times, even though the number of

carry electrical signals, called nerve impulses, which can be passed on to other neurons. This constant buzz of signals around the body is what allows you to think, feel, and move. The neurons themselves consist

SOME NERVE IMPULSES TRAVEL AT UP TO 400 KMH (250 MPH)

neurons stays about the same. So what do these neurons look like, and what do they do?

N eurons and nerves

Glad you asked! What makes neurons unique is that they can

of a cell body (an expanded bit with a nucleus inside) sprouting lots of branches called dendrites, which receive signals from other neurons. From the other side of the cell body emerges a sort of "tail",

18

LOG ON...
www.soton.ac.uk/
~jrc3/chudler/neurok.html

called an axon or nerve fibre. The axon carries nerve impulses on to the next neuron. Axons are often very short, but in some neurons (such as those running between the spinal cord and the big toe) they can be up to 1 m (3.3 ft) long.

There are three main groups of neurons: 1. association neurons pass on and sort impulses inside the brain and spinal cord – the central nervous system (or CNS); 2. sensory neurons carry messages from sensors, such as those in the skin or eye, to the CNS; 3. motor neurons carry signals from the CNS to your muscles, instructing them to contract and make you move. Outside the CNS, these motor and sensory neurons are bound together in pale, glistening cables called nerves. These sprout from the brain and spinal cord and travel to every part of the body.

Nerve impulses
The first hint that messages were carried by nerves

in the form of electrical signals came in the 18th century. In the 1780s, Luigi Galvani (1737–98), an Italian professor of anatomy at the University of Bologna, was investigating the contraction of the muscles in frogs' legs. One day, while dissecting a frog on an iron plate, he touched the frog with a brass hook and was surprised to see its leg twitch. Galvani concluded that "animal electricity" produced inside the frog had made its leg muscles contract and twitch. He also suggested that this "animal electricity" was generated in the brain, carried by the nerves, and stored in muscles until it was needed. Good guess, but wrong! Galvani's "animal electricity" doesn't exist, but he was right that something electrical was

THE NERVOUS SYSTEM IS MADE UP OF THE BRAIN, THE SPINAL CORD, A NETWORK OF NERVES, AND THE SENSES.

Fast-action squid

But why do some animals, like the squid (and, indeed, its cousin the octopus), have giant axons? Well, the wider the axon, the faster the speed at which the impulse travels. In the squid's case, its giant nerve fibres transmit impulses to the muscles that control rapid movement, as well as to those in charge of its tentacles. This enables the squid to make a rapid exit when danger threatens, and to shoot out its tentacles with lightning-fast speed to capture passing prey.

involved. We now know that a resting neuron is rather like a battery, with an electrical charge across its membrane (outer skin). When the neuron is stimulated – we'll come to how this happens later – the charge suddenly reverses, producing an electrical signal that races along the axon (the long "tail" of the neuron). This high-speed signal is what we call a nerve impulse.

Giant axons

There doesn't seem to be an obvious connection between squid and nerve impulses, but there is. These marine animals are molluscs, the animal group that also includes snails and slugs. Unlike their slow-moving land relatives, squid have giant axons. They're called "giant" because at 1 mm (0.04 in) across they're 50 times wider than a normal axon. This makes them useful for scientists trying to find out how nerve impulses travel along neurons.

ENDS OF AXON
CONNECT
WITH OTHER
NEURONS.

MYELIN SHEATH

AXON

THIS MOTOR
NEURON HAS A CELL
BODY WITH LOTS OF
DENDRITES, AND A
LONG AXON, OR
NERVE FIBRE.

20

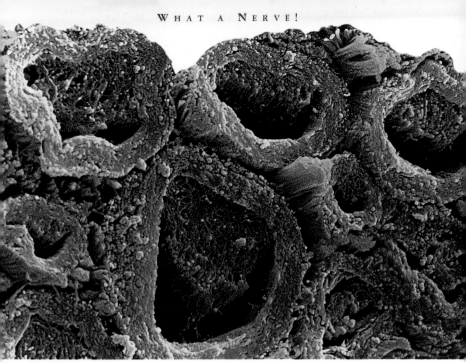

I nsulated for speed

So, do we humans have giant axons? No, we don't. If we did, there wouldn't be room enough to pack in all the billions of neurons that we need to make us behave the way we do. In that case, if we don't have giant fibres, why don't we crawl around at a snail's pace? The

THIS SLICE THROUGH A NERVE REVEALS BUNDLES OF AXONS (GREEN). EACH BUNDLE IS SURROUNDED BY A TOUGH, PROTECTIVE SHEATH (MAUVE).

answer is that many of our axons are wrapped in a fatty coat called a myelin sheath, which insulates the axons and helps them to transmit nerve impulses more quickly. These axons, although much thinner than a squid's, carry nerve impulses at up to 100 m (328 ft) per second – five times faster than the marine mollusc's.

B ridging the gap

When Camillo Golgi examined the nerve cells he'd discovered, back in the 1870s, he believed

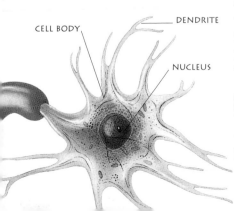

CELL BODY

DENDRITE

NUCLEUS

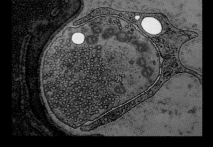

that they were linked tightly together in a continuous network. But not everyone agreed. In Spain, the anatomist Santiago Ramón y Cajal (1852–1934) thought that neurons were separate units that lay very close to each other. It was only in the 1960s that the electron microscope, with its amazing powers of magnification, showed that Ramón y Cajal was right.

Neurons meet at a junction called a synapse, where there is a tiny gap between one neuron and the the next. When a nerve impulse reaches the end of an axon, it releases a chemical, called a neurotransmitter. This crosses the

gap and, just 1 millisecond later, stimulates the neuron on the other side of the synapse and sets off a nerve impulse within it. It's a bit like you running along a straight road and finding there's a narrow but deep stretch of water, so you have to launch a boat to reach the other side and then carry on running.

Nerve poisons
Ever wondered why the venom, or poison, of some animals is so dangerous? Well, animals such as black widow spiders and poison dart frogs produce

THE SKIN OF THIS POISON DART FROG PRODUCES A DEADLY NERVE CHEMICAL THAT PARALYZES ITS ENEMIES.

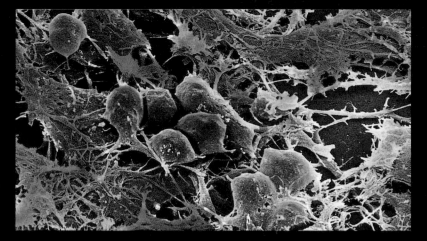

GLIAL CELLS LIKE THESE (BLUE) HOLD THE NERVOUS SYSTEM TOGETHER, AND SUPPORT AND FEED THE MESSAGE-CARRYING NEURONS.

venom or secretions containing chemicals called neurotoxins. These chemicals interfere with the release of neurotransmitters, so that the nervous system goes out of control. If this happens, a person's breathing and heart rate can be affected and they can die. Nerve gases used in warfare work in a similar way.

Holding it all together

But neurons aren't the only type of cells in the nervous system. A massive supporting cast of glial cells play vital roles, even though they don't themselves carry nerve impulses. In fact, in the brain alone there are one trillion glial cells – ten times the number of neurons. Glial cells appear to

stick on to neurons, so it's not surprising that they get their name from *glia*, the Greek word for glue. As well as supporting neurons and holding them together – and forming an insulating sheath around some neurons – glial cells also supply neurons with food and repair any damage. Some even wander around gobbling up any lurking bacteria or debris from damaged cells. Together, neurons and their "glue cells" make the nervous system work.

WEIRD WORLD
FOREST DWELLERS IN TROPICAL SOUTH AMERICA USE THE NEUROTOXINS FROM POISON-DART FROGS TO TIP THEIR ARROWS. PREY SHOT DURING HUNTS IS PARALYZED IN SECONDS.

MAPPING THE BRAIN

If you visit somewhere new, the best way to explore it is to use a map. In the same way, doctors need "maps" of the body to help them treat patients. For years, scientists have been trying to map the brain by finding out which parts of the brain do what. But it has taken a long time. The story begins with an Austrian doctor named Franz Gall, who had some rather strange ideas.

Feel the bumps

Press your fingers on your head and feel your skull. You'll find that it's not entirely smooth, but has little bumps on it. Franz Gall (1758–1828) had a theory about this. He reckoned that the brain was made up of many different parts, each of which was in charge of a different aspect of personality. For example, he thought that if someone had a good sense of humour, the "humour" part of their brain would bulge outwards. Gall believed that the brain bulges produced bumps on the skull. By feeling these bumps, he

A PHRENOLOGY HEAD SHOWED WHICH PARTS OF THE SKULL – AND THUS THE BRAIN – WERE SUPPOSED TO CONTROL DIFFERENT ASPECTS OF PERSONALITY.

thought that he could tell what someone's personality was like, and even identify people who were likely to become criminals.

To test this, Gall examined the skulls of executed criminals and tried to match personalities to bumps. Many skulls later, he had matched 32 characteristics to different regions of the skull. His theory, called phrenology, really took off. It was as popular (and just as unscientific) in the early 19th century as horoscopes are today. Some people bought phrenology heads marked with Gall's regions so they could test their own bumps. Others went to a phrenology expert to "have their head examined".

PIERRE PAUL BROCA (ABOVE) DISCOVERED THAT A SMALL AREA ON THE LEFT SIDE OF THE BRAIN CONTROLS SPEECH – NOT AN AREA UNDER THE EYE, AS GALL AND THE PHRENOLOGISTS HAD THOUGHT.

QUEEN VICTORIA SENT HER CHILDREN TO A PHRENOLOGIST

Speech control

French doctor Pierre Paul Broca (1824–80) saw absolutely no link between bumps and brains. Broca was interested in patients who couldn't speak properly because they had brain damage. In 1861, Broca examined a patient who was nicknamed Tan because whatever he was asked he always replied with the word "tan". Six days later, Tan died. Broca removed Tan's brain and found that an area of the brain – on the left-hand side towards the front – was damaged. After examining the brains of other people with similar speech problems, Broca concluded that this part of the brain (now called Broca's area) was responsible for producing speech.

In 1874, Karl Wernicke (1848–1905), another Austrian doctor, discovered a second area of the brain concerned

25

with speech. It was also on the left side of the brain, but not so far forward. Wernicke's area, as it came to be called, makes sure we choose the right words when we speak. Wernicke found that his brain-damaged patients could speak perfectly well – they just talked complete nonsense!

Phrenology was already on the way out when Broca and Wernicke did their work. By identifying the areas of the brain that controlled speech and language, the two scientists finally finished phrenology off.

Scans and probes

Broca and Wernicke had to wait until their patients were dead before they could take a look at their brains. That's not the case for today's scientists and doctors. They can use high-tech devices to explore the brains of living patients. A machine called a CT scanner uses X-rays and a computer to produce images like the ones on pages 12 and 68. MRI scanners are used a lot to produce detailed pictures of the inside of the brain. A PET scanner records brain activity by showing which parts of the brain "light up" on a computer screen when a person is reading a book, listening to music, and so on.

Another tool used by some brain-mapping scientists is the electrode – a fine metal needle that can probe into different parts of the living brain. (If this sounds painful, it isn't – the brain can't feel any pain as it doesn't have any pain sensors.) An electric current is passed through an electrode to an area of the brain, and the person is asked what he or she feels or experiences. That's how we know, for example, which bit of the brain tells your fingers to move, or lets you feel your feet being tickled.

reading this page, listening to music, solving a problem, feeling pain, creating a painting, learning a language, or just being yourself, your cerebrum's in control.

LOG ON...
Probe the brain at www.pbs.org/wgbh/aso/tryit/brain

THIS PET SCAN SHOWS WHICH PARTS OF THE BRAIN ARE ACTIVE WHEN A PERSON IS THINKING AND SPEAKING.

B iggest part

So far, we've talked about the brain as if it's just one lump of tissue. But it's actually made up of different sections – but not in the way that Franz Gall thought. The biggest brain section is the cerebrum. Whether you're

To be more precise, it's the thin layer, just 2 mm (0.08 in) thick, around the outside of the cerebrum that's in charge of all the things that make you a thinking, intelligent human being. This layer is the cerebral cortex, or grey matter. The cortex may be thin but it's very wrinkly, which means that much more of it can be packed into the skull. You can see this if you crumple up a piece of paper.

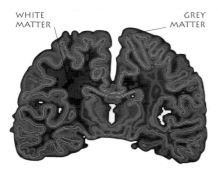

WHITE MATTER

GREY MATTER

THIS MRI SCAN SHOWS A VERTICAL SLICE THROUGH THE BRAIN, WITH A LAYER OF GREY MATTER (CEREBRAL CORTEX) ON THE OUTSIDE AND WHITE MATTER INSIDE.

It fits into a much smaller space than when it was flat. Having a large cortex is what separates us from our nearest but less-smart relatives. Spread out the cortex of a chimp and it would cover an A4 piece of paper. Your own cortex would cover an area four times bigger.

Cortex areas

As far as mapping the cortex is concerned, scientists have clear ideas about some areas but not others. The sensory areas receive a stream of nerve impulses from the eyes, ears, skin, and so on, allowing you to see, hear, and feel. The motor areas send out instructions to muscles, making them contract to move your body. But large chunks, called association areas, are not so well mapped. They link motor and sensory areas – enabling you to run away if you spot a charging elephant – but they are also involved in activities such as remembering, thinking, and imagining, as well as giving you your own personality.

Left and right

If you look at the photo on page 26, you'll notice that the cerebrum is divided into two halves, or hemispheres. Rather surprisingly, the left hemisphere is in charge of the

IF AN ELEPHANT CHARGED TOWARDS YOU, YOUR BRAIN WOULD ACT ON THE INFORMATION, MAKING YOU RUN AWAY!

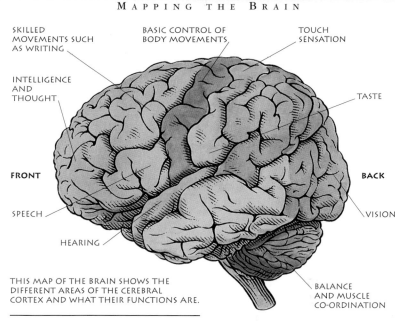

SKILLED MOVEMENTS SUCH AS WRITING

BASIC CONTROL OF BODY MOVEMENTS

TOUCH SENSATION

INTELLIGENCE AND THOUGHT

TASTE

FRONT

BACK

SPEECH

VISION

HEARING

BALANCE AND MUSCLE CO-ORDINATION

THIS MAP OF THE BRAIN SHOWS THE DIFFERENT AREAS OF THE CEREBRAL CORTEX AND WHAT THEIR FUNCTIONS ARE.

right side of the body, while the right hemisphere controls the body's left side. So, if you put your left hand in icy water, your right hemisphere will register "cold". And if you want to move your right foot, your left hemisphere will send out instructions telling your right leg's muscles to do their job.

The two hemispheres also have more general functions. The left hemisphere is usually in charge of language (both spoken and written), scientific and number skills, and problem solving. The right hemisphere specializes in imagination, "spatial" skills (those you need, for example,

to build something or navigate), and the appreciation of art and music. The left hemisphere is usually dominant, which is why most people are right-handed.

THE LEFT SIDE OF THIS US FOOTBALLER'S BRAIN CONTROLS HIS RIGHT HAND AS HE PREPARES TO THROW THE BALL.

THE LIMBIC SYSTEM (SHOWN IN BLUE ON THIS DIAGRAM) IS A CLUSTER OF BRAIN STRUCTURES THAT PLAYS A VITAL ROLE IN EMOTIONS AND MEMORY.

CEREBRAL CORTEX

LIMBIC SYSTEM

CEREBELLUM

PART OF BRAIN STEM

S plit brain

A band of nerve fibres called the corpus callosum links the two halves of the brain so that they can constantly and instantly swap information. Doctors may cut through the corpus callosum go their own way. One woman found that it took much longer to get dressed. As her right hand (controlled by her left hemisphere) took one item of clothing from the wardrobe, her right hemisphere told her

RIGHT-HANDERS OUTNUMBER LEFT-HANDERS BY NINE TO ONE

to stop people with epilepsy experiencing fits. Although the two hemispheres can no longer communicate, most people who have had this operation can still lead normal lives. However, for a few people, the separated hemispheres seem to want to left hand to put it back and choose another one. She said it was like having two naughty children fighting in her head!

G etting emotional

Tucked away between the lower parts of the two cerebral

hemispheres are the brain parts that make up the limbic system. If you've ever found that a certain smell brings back a really strong memory, you've experienced the limbic system at work. Similarly, the fear that some people feel when they see a hairy spider is also the limbic system's fault. As well as helping us recall memories, processing smells, and making us scared, the limbic system produces many other emotions, including anger, disappointment, pleasure, sadness, and hope.

Movers and shakers

Two other brain sections need mentioning. The brain stem is

CHARACTERS IN THE FILM THE MUMMY ARE SHOWING FEAR – AN EMOTION PRODUCED BY THE BRAIN'S LIMBIC SYSTEM.

the stalk-like part that the limbic system sits on. It acts like the body's "autopilot", always keeping your breathing and heartbeat at the right rate – slow when you're just lying in front of the TV, and fast when you're running for a bus. The brain stem also connects to the spinal cord, providing a vital link between your brain and all the nerves that fan out to every part of the body.

Shaped like a cauliflower, the cerebellum sticks out from below the back of the cerebrum. Its job is to make you move in a smooth, co-ordinated way and to keep you balanced, whether you are performing a pirouette or just walking down the street. The brain stem and cerebellum complete our tour of the brain.

IT'S ALL IN THE MIND

Look in a mirror. What do you see? A human being who you recognize as being you. Each waking second, we are aware that we're alive, have a sense of "self", and know that there's a past, present, and future. This awareness, called consciousness, is produced by our mind. Having a mind is unique to humans…or is it?

Artificial minds

Ever since the first computers were built in the late 1940s, scientists have dreamt of making an artificial thinking, feeling brain. They've also wanted to equip it with a synthetic body to create a walking, talking, human-like robot.

The reality today is that, yes, there are lots of robots, but most don't look much like us. You find them on factory production lines doing boring, repetitive jobs that people don't want to do. It's difficult enough to get robots to move like us, let alone think like us. Some scientists think ever-more powerful computers may one day enable artificial brains to mimic human brains. Others

THIS ROBOT CAN WALK AND CLIMB STAIRS, BUT IT DOESN'T HAVE A BRAIN AND CAN'T THINK.

ASIMO

HONDA

claim that this is impossible, because no machine could ever imitate the workings of the complex network of nerve cells in a living brain.

Mind and personality

For hundreds of years, people thought that the brain really did work like a machine, receiving instructions from a mind located somewhere outside the body, like a radio picking up radio waves. These days we know that the mind is very much part of the brain and its activities. But what do we mean by mind? Well, a person's "mind" is made up of attitudes, intelligence, feelings, reactions, manners, and much more. All these features of the mind differ slightly from one person to another, giving each of us a unique personality.

Testing times

Is it possible to describe a person's personality accurately? You might say that someone is generous or mean, pleasant or unpleasant, but that's just your opinion. Psychologists (scientists who study the brain and behaviour) have created tests that try to reveal people's

THE WORD PERSONALITY COMES FROM THE LATIN "PERSONA" – THE WORD FOR THE MASK WORN BY ROMAN ACTORS TO SHOW WHICH CHARACTER THEY WERE PLAYING.

personalities. Some tests ask questions. Others get people to make up a story to fit a picture. In the Rorschach test, people have to say what symmetrical inkblots resemble. Do they look like objects, people, or animals?

them with what you are experiencing now, so that you can make sense of the world. Short-term memory deals with "now", and lets you briefly recall a phone number or avoid walking into a tree you've just noticed.

INKBLOTS LIKE THIS ARE USED IN THE RORSCHACH TEST. WHAT DO THE SHAPES LOOK LIKE TO YOU?

Psychologists use a person's answers to learn more about his or her personality.

Thanks for the memory

Shaping your personality are a lot of brain features unique to you, including your memory, intelligence, ability to learn, and imagination. Thanks to your memory, not only can you recall events, facts, and faces from the past, but you can also compare

Short-term memories worth keeping (the brain forgets most of them quickly) get shunted around until they pass into long-term memory, which holds them for months, years, or a lifetime.

In the long term

Long-term memories take several forms, such as recalling facts and figures or remembering

MEMORIES OF IMPORTANT EVENTS, SUCH AS A SPECIAL PARTY, CAN LAST MANY YEARS.

skilled movements like riding a bike. The memories are stored in different parts of the cerebral cortex, probably as a pattern of connections between neurons.

Remembering everyday events, like going on holiday or seeing a film, uses another type of long-term memory. Daily happenings that the brain wants to keep are held in its limbic system. The limbic system regularly replays the experiences "upstairs" to the cortex, where they eventually go into long-term storage. Much of this replaying occurs at night. You may be familiar with it – it's called dreaming!

INSTRUCTIONS HELD IN THE LONG-TERM MEMORY HELP THIS CYCLIST TO PERFORM BREATH-TAKING STUNTS.

F ears and phobias

Do you shudder at the sight of a hairy spider, or quake at the sight of a snake? Once again, your memory is responsible – this time it's the "fears" memory in your limbic system. Some fears are "built-in" to our brains, passed down from our ancestors, who had every reason to fear

poisonous snakes and spiders. For most of us, once we realize that an object or situation is harmless, our fear disappears.

Some people have phobias – intense and irrational fears that are set off by all sorts of things and don't go away. It could be a fear of objects such as birds (ornithophobia), or a situation such as flying (aviophobia).

There are literally hundreds of phobias. Why do people get them? Possibly because they were brought up by someone with similar fears, or because they had a bad experience that they associated with the object or event. Luckily, many people with phobias are able to get help.

HERE'S SOMEONE WHO OBVIOUSLY DOESN'T SUFFER FROM ACROPHOBIA, THE FEAR OF HEIGHTS.

Lifetime learning

Do you remember learning to walk? Probably not, because you were too young when it happened. But walking is one of millions of things that we learn in our lifetime. And of course, without our memory, learning would be impossible. Things like walking, writing, or riding a bike are learned by a process called trial and error. You try something out using certain muscles, remember where you went wrong or right, and then improve the activity the next time you try it.

But there are other ways of learning. Repeated use of words or numbers transfers them into your cerebral cortex so they can be recalled later. That's how you are able to do maths

WE LEARN TO WALK BY REPEATEDLY TRYING TO BALANCE WHILE TAKING A FEW STEPS.

How intelligent?

Another aspect of personality is intelligence. This appears to be a combination of many things, including the ability to recall memories, creativity, ease of

PARASKAVEDEKATRIAPHOBIA IS A FEAR OF FRIDAY THE 13TH

or learn a language.

A third type of learning involves insight and reasoning. Learning to play chess, for example, requires an ability to draw on previous experiences as well as having the ideas and strategy to plan future moves on the chess board.

learning, planning skills, use of words, and problem-solving powers. Scientists think that in all there are up to 120 different aspects of intelligence.

Mind reading

Most scientists think that the "mind reading" feats of some stage performers are just tricks.

ALPHA WAVES – PRODUCED WHEN AWAKE BUT RESTING

BETA WAVES – PRODUCED WHEN ALERT AND CONCENTRATING

DELTA WAVES – PRODUCED IN DEEP SLEEP

THESE PATTERNS PRODUCED BY AN EEG MACHINE SHOW THREE DIFFERENT TYPES OF BRAIN WAVE.

However, one way in which scientists can read minds is with an electroencephalogram (EEG). This records brain waves produced by the constant stream of electrical signals passing between the neurons. These fuzzy patterns can't actually show what a person is thinking, but they do indicate how alert he or she is.

Sleep and hypnosis

So far we've thought about the active, conscious mind that is aware of everything going on around it. But what happens to it when we go to sleep? Does the mind "switch off"? Well, no it doesn't, and we know this from using EEGs. Brain waves taken from a sleeping person show that they go into a deep sleep first, then into a light sleep (called REM sleep) when they are nearly awake,

THIS MAN IS CONNECTED TO AN EEG MACHINE BY A HOST OF WIRES AND ELECTRODES (METAL PLATES).

then back into deep sleep. This is repeated through the night with the periods of REM sleep getting longer. It's during REM sleep that we dream.

Someone who's asleep isn't unconscious because they can easily be woken up by, say, a loud sound. Sleep is a period of altered consciousness, and so, in its own way, is hypnosis. Listening to a repeated phrase, a hypnotized person goes into a trance-like state in which they are much more open to suggestion. Hypnosis is often used to help people stop smoking or overcome phobias.

Mind problems
Unfortunately, hypnosis isn't much help for most problems affecting the mind. Illnesses can affect the brain, just as they do

18TH-CENTURY ASYLUMS WERE BRUTAL PLACES, WHERE MENTALLY-ILL PEOPLE WERE RIDICULED AND CRUELLY TREATED.

other parts of the body. The difference is that they change the way people feel, think, and behave. For centuries, people with mental illnesses (as they are called) were treated very badly because of their "odd" behaviour, and were locked away in prison-like asylums.

In the 19th century, hospitals were set up where mentally ill people could be treated. And a new science, psychiatry, was established to investigate mental illnesses, their causes, and their treatment. Today we know that many mental problems are in fact caused by an unusual brain structure, or by an imbalance in brain chemicals that can be successfully treated by drugs.

SENSING THE WORLD

H ow does your brain find out what's happening in the outside world? By using the senses of touch, vision, hearing, smell, and taste. These five senses detect any changes in your surroundings, and send messages hurtling to your brain to keep it constantly updated about what's going on. Without senses, not only would the world be a very, very dull place, but we simply wouldn't survive in it.

Common sensors

The flash of a camera, a clap of thunder, the prick of a thorn – these are just a few things that our senses detect. But just how do our body's senses work? The answer is through tiny structures called sensors. There are several types of sensor. Each type reacts to something different that we experience, such as light, sound, or touch, by firing off a nerve impulse. Any change

LIGHTNING AND THUNDER ARE STIMULI THAT ACTIVATE OUR SENSES.

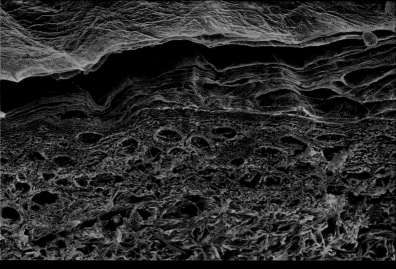

in the outside world that makes a sensor send an impulse zipping along nerve fibres to the brain is called a stimulus (or stimuli, if there's more than one).

Some sensors, such as those for touch, are scattered over the body's surface. Others are grouped together in special sense organs, such as the eyes (packed with light sensors) and the ears (full of sound sensors).

Do you react to every single stimulus your sensors pick up? No, thank goodness! Many messages from the sensors get "filtered out" by part of the brain stem. Without this filter, your brain – or to be more precise, your cerebral cortex – would be overwhelmed by incoming data. You wouldn't, for example, be able to read this book, because you'd be constantly distracted by

THE DERMIS (THE YELLOW LAYER IN THIS MAGNIFIED CROSS-SECTION THROUGH THE SKIN) CONTAINS MOST OF THE SKIN'S SENSORS. IT LIES UNDER A PROTECTIVE LAYER CALLED THE EPIDERMIS (PINK/RED).

what's happening around you.

To start our tour of the senses, let's look at the sense of touch, as well as some unusual senses found in other animals but not in humans. You'll find the other senses – smell, taste, hearing, and vision, in later chapters.

Skin sensors

We take our sense of touch for granted. But think about it – just by feeling with your fingertips you can, without looking, tell the difference between soft velvet or rough sandpaper. It's amazing, and it's all down to millions of touch sensors in the skin – the waterproof,

41

USING THE BRAILLE SYSTEM, A BLIND PERSON IS ABLE TO "READ" BY FEELING PATTERNS OF RAISED DOTS WITH THEIR FINGERTIPS.

dry. The feedback from the sensors also enables the brain to calculate how hard the fingers can grip objects without either dropping or squashing them.

Sensitive regions

The millions of sensors are not spread evenly over your skin. You won't be surprised to hear that the areas with the highest concentration of sensors are your fingertips, lips, and tongue. Many blind people learn to use

germproof protective layer that covers your body. The sensors nearest to the skin's surface are triggered by the lightest of touches. Others, found deeper in the skin, need to be squeezed

SENSOR'S NEAR THE SKIN'S SURFACE PRODUCE ITCHES AND TICKLES

out of shape by vibrations or heavy pressure before they fire off their nerve impulses.

The information that arrives at the brain from these different sensors allows it to produce a "touch map" of the body's surroundings. This tells the brain, from second to second, which parts of the body are in contact with surfaces that are hard or soft, rough or smooth, still or vibrating, or wet or

their sensitive fingertips to "read" using the Braille system, in which patterns of raised dots represent letters and numbers. Skin regions with the fewest sensors include your back and neck.

Wherever they are located, these sensors for touch and pressure send information to the sensory part of the cerebral cortex. The parts of the sensory cortex that deal with the most sensitive areas of

MOST OF THE TIME WE'RE NOT AWARE OF OUR CLOTHES AGAINST OUR SKIN.

skin, like the fingertips, are much bigger than those dealing with the least sensitive ones, such as the back.

L osing touch

If you keep stimulating the same sensors, the brain will eventually start to ignore the messages coming from them. For example, when you first put your clothes on, they rub against your skin and trigger the touch sensors. Although the sensors continue firing off their signals, your brain pays no attention to them after a while. If it didn't do this, you'd spend the whole day feeling uncomfortable and itchy – so well-done brain! This process is called habituation, a word that simply means "getting used to".

F eel the heat

There are more than just touch and pressure sensors in the skin. Stand under an icy shower or run into the freezing sea and instantly find out how cold it is. Similarly, if you put your hand into a hot bath, you soon know

whether it is too hot to get into. Heat sensors are found near the surface of the skin. They help you avoid harm from extreme heat or cold. But heat sensors soon adapt to their surroundings. That's why you can feel very chilly when you first stand under a cold shower, but you soon get used to it. And they can be deceptive as well. Put your hand in very cold water for a minute or two, then put it into water at room temperature. You'll find that the room-temperature water feels warm!

P ainful experience

If you accidentally stand on a pin or shut your finger in a door, some of the 3 million or so pain sensors in your skin tell you immediately that you're hurt. Anything piercing or pinching

LOG ON...
http://faculty.washington.edu/chudler/chtouch.html

TEMPERATURE SENSORS TELL THESE SWIMMERS WHETHER THE WATER'S WARM OR COLD.

THIS SOCCER PLAYER FEELS
AGONIZING PAIN AS SENSORS
WARN HIS BRAIN THAT DAMAGE
HAS OCCURRED TO HIS LEG.

the skin causes the release of chemicals that stimulate pain sensors. The sensors shoot off nerve impulses to the brain, and – "Ouch!" – you feel a sharp pain. There are also pain sensors in many places inside the body, which usually produce a dull, aching pain. Stomach-ache is just one example of these inner pain sensors at work. Whether they're on the surface or inside your body, all pain sensors perform the valuable service of sounding the alarm that part of you is being damaged.

By the way, one of the few body parts not to have any pain sensors is the brain! So how do headaches happen? The answer is through tension in the skull muscles and irritation of the protective layers – the meninges – that surround the brain.

Remarkably, there are times when people are badly injured but don't feel pain. For example, some soldiers have told of how they were shot or cut but felt nothing at all. That's because, under the stress of battle, the body produces chemicals that act as natural painkillers. Once the fighting is over, however, the pain begins.

On the other hand, some people who have had a limb

amputated (cut off) can still feel pains and itches in the missing part, even though it's no longer there! Called "phantom pain", it's thought to happen because severed nerve fibres in the remains of the limb continue to send impulses back to the brain. The brain is tricked into thinking that the rest of the arm or leg is still there.

F eeling their way

Look at your arm and you'll see that it's covered with fine hairs. These, like the thicker hairs on your head, grow from tube-like pits deep in the skin called follicles. Now, carefully stroke the hairs on your arm without touching the skin. You should

feel a very slight sensation of touch. The reason for this is that at the bottom of each follicle is a tiny touch sensor. When you stroke the hair, the sensor sends messages to the brain that give you a feeling of being touched.

This "hairy" sense may not seem very important to us, but it's invaluable to some of our mammal relatives, such as cats. Cats are nocturnal (active at night) and their whiskers help them to navigate in the dark. These long hairs enable cats to judge the width of openings and avoid obstacles. They also curve forward when a cat is

TWO HAIRS EMERGE FROM SKIN FOLLICLES. THE ROOTS OF THE HAIRS ARE LINKED TO TINY TOUCH SENSORS.

MIGRATING GEESE USE THE EARTH'S MAGNETIC FIELD TO HELP THEM REACH THE RIGHT DESTINATION.

about to pounce on prey. The tips of the whiskers hit the prey first, and instantaneously tell the cat precisely when and where to deliver the killing bite. Look out for this whisker curling next time you see a cat being fed – not on live prey, but while it's waiting for a can of cat food to be opened.

It's not only mammals that use projections from their bodies to navigate. Many insects, such as cave crickets, use their long antennae to feel their way in the dark. The antennae can also detect vibrations in the air.

Electricity and magnetism

Some animals use senses that we just don't have. Take the duck-billed platypus of Australia, for example. This water-loving mammal grubs around on the bottom of streams in search of tasty morsels such as crayfish and insect larvae. It can't see much in the murky water, but its duck-like bill has sensors that detect tiny electrical signals produced by the bodies of its prey. It uses these signals to home in on its victims. Sharks have the same ability. Weak electrical signals picked up by sensors under the snout lead these ocean hunters to their next meal.

A CAT'S WHISKERS CURVE FORWARDS AS IT PREPARES TO POUNCE ON ITS PREY.

Another thing that humans (probably) aren't sensitive to is magnetism. The Earth acts like a big bar magnet (the sort used in experiments at school) and has its own gigantic magnetic field. It seems that some birds, and other living things, can sense magnetism. They use the Earth's magnetic field to help them navigate on the long journeys they make each year to new breeding or feeding grounds. These journeys are called migrations.

WEIRD WORLD
SOME ANIMALS ARE ATTRACTED BY HEAT. EUROPEAN JEWEL BEETLES FLY TOWARDS FOREST FIRES AND LAY THEIR EGGS ON WARM TREE BARK TO GIVE THEM THE BEST CHANCE OF DEVELOPING.

SHARKS USE ELECTRICAL SENSORS TO PINPOINT PREY AT CLOSE RANGE. THEY ALSO HAVE SENSORS TO DETECT VIBRATIONS IN WATER.

Feel that smell!

You may not be able to pick up electrical signals from your friends, or tell which direction is north without looking at a compass, but have you ever smelled a particular odour when you heard a certain sound? If you have, you may be the one person in every 25,000 that experiences synaesthesia, which means "sensations together". This is the ability of the brain to mix two or more senses, so that you can, for example, "smell" sounds or "hear" colours.

Some scientists think that all of us do this when we're very young, but we usually lose the ability as we get older. Other scientists see it as evidence that there's communication between the different sensory regions of the cerebral cortex, and that our senses are linked in some way. Regardless of whether you can smell sounds, let's see how smell – and its close relative taste – actually work.

SMELLS AND TASTES

Mealtimes would be much less tempting if we couldn't smell the aroma of freshly cooked food. And they'd be positively boring if all food tasted the same or, worse still, of nothing. Thanks to your nose and tongue, your brain is kept informed about all incoming odours and tastes. But there's more to taste and smell than just helping you to enjoy life – they can also keep you out of danger.

Nice or nasty?

Both smell and taste detect chemicals, either floating in the air (smell) or in food and drink (taste). Of these two senses, smell is the most important, as it is about 20,000 times more sensitive than taste. As well as detecting pleasant odours like food, flowers, and perfume, your sense of smell also gives an early warning against possible danger. The smell of smoke, for example, tells your brain that something's burning, while the stench of rotten food warns

OUR NOSES ACT LIKE FIRE ALARMS, ALERTING US TO THE DANGER OF FIRE AS SOON AS SMOKE IS DETECTED.

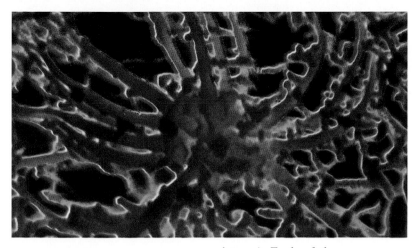

THIS MICROSCOPIC SMELL SENSOR, WITH ITS MANY BRANCHES, IS ONE OF MANY MILLIONS IN THE NASAL CAVITY.

you not eat it. However, you soon get used to, and ignore, most odours within a matter of minutes. That's why someone working in a sewage plant – phew! – can eat their lunch without feeling ill. But, whether they are nice or nasty, how do you actually smell smells?

Odour detectors

Imagine if you were small – and brave – enough to climb up someone's nostril. Once you'd pushed your way through the nose hairs (yuk!), you would emerge in the cave-like nasal cavity. The roof of this cavity is packed with smell sensors – about 25 million in all – and covered by watery mucus (mucus is the stuff that makes saliva a bit more thick and dripty). Each of these sensors, called a receptor cell, carries 20 or so scent-detecting "hairs".

Whenever you breathe in or sniff, scent molecules (particles) in the air dissolve in the mucus. The molecules stick onto the sensory hairs. This makes the the receptor cells blast messages off to the brain so that it can identify the particular odour. What's really interesting is that these messages are routed through the limbic system. Remember, this is a part of the

A RING-TAILED LEMUR IN MADAGASCAR
RUBS ITS REAR END AGAINST A TREE TO
LEAVE A SCENT FOR OTHER LEMURS.

brain involved in memory and emotions. That's why certain smells can spark off really intense memories. On the other hand, a smell associated with danger, such as smoke, can produce a feeling of fear that makes us want to run away.

S niffer dogs

In a "Who's got the best sense of smell?" competition, dogs would easily beat us. Their noses have 10 times as many receptor cells as our own. Not only can dogs pick up many more scents than us, but they can also detect smells that are far too weak for us to notice. In the wild, this amazing sense of smell allows dogs to follow faint scent trails left by prey. Humans put this ability to good use by training dogs to sniff out illegal drugs or explosives at airports.

OUR SENSE OF SMELL IS
FEEBLE COMPARED
TO A DOG'S.

L eaving a message

Dogs also use their great sense of smell to pick up messages left by other dogs when they urinate on trees and lamp-posts. Take any dog for a walk, and it will soon start sniffing out the "chemical notes" left by other dogs…and then no doubt leave a reply of its own!

It's not just dogs that use scent for communication. Cats, such as African cheetahs, regularly mark trees and rocks on the boundary of their territory with sprays of urine. This chemical message could say "Keep out!" to a rival, or "Shall we have a family?" to a potential mate. The messages are carried by chemicals in the urine called pheromones.

Pheromones are also found in the insect world. Some female moths release airborne trails of pheromone molecules that can attract male moths from many kilometres away. One scientist spilled an artificial version of the pheromone on his clothes. When he went out at night, he found himself mobbed by hordes of love-sick male moths!

R are birds

Unlike us hairy mammals, our feathered friends the birds have a poor sense of smell. They rely instead on their superb eyesight to find food, mates, and so on. But there are a few exceptions, such as New Zealand's kiwi. This flightless bird's nostrils are found, rather unusually, at the end of its long bill (most birds' nostrils are at the top of the bill, near the eyes). The kiwi hunts at night for worms, beetles, and other juicy items

by sticking the tip of its sensitive bill into the soil to sniff out prey. Another odour-loving bird is the turkey vulture of the Americas. Like other vultures, it feeds on carrion (dead animals). Unlike its relatives, it finds lunch not by sight but by sniffing the wind for the smell of rotting meat.

T he smell of home

Could you use your sense of smell to find your way home – perhaps following the filthy reek of some dirty socks under the bed? Of course not. Well, some fish can (okay, they don't follow smelly socks!). Take salmon, for example. These fish hatch out from their eggs and develop in streams. Once they're big enough, the salmon swim downstream until they reach a

LOG ON...
www.hmce.gov.uk/
public/how/sniffer-dogs.htm

THESE TURKEY VULTURES ARE WAITING FOR A WHIFF OF ROTTING FLESH THAT WILL GUIDE THEM TO THEIR NEXT MEAL.

river, which they follow to the sea. They spend the next few years feeding in the ocean. When the time comes for them to breed, they return to the river and swim back up it. But how do they pick out their own stream from the many that run into the river? The answer is that they use their incredible sense of smell to detect the tiny scent traces in the water that identify a particular stream as "home".

A flick of the tongue

If you've ever watched snakes or lizards, you'll have noticed them flicking their tongues in and out. They do this to pick up scents in the air to help them follow prey, find a mate, sample food, or avoid enemies. Chemicals are drawn in from the air and passed from the tip of the tongue to a cavity in the roof of the mouth called the Jacobson's organ. Here, sensory cells partly smell and partly taste whatever arrives.

Good taste

Luckily, we don't have to stick our tongues out to detect tastes and smells, otherwise we would upset a lot of people! But if you do flick out your tongue while looking in a mirror, you'll see that it's covered with lots of tiny bumps, called papillae. The sides of the papillae are studded with sensors called taste buds. There are about 10,000 taste buds on your tongue. Despite being so numerous, the sensors detect just four different tastes – salty, sweet, sour, and bitter.

When food arrives in the mouth, some of it dissolves in saliva. As it washes over the taste buds, they relay messages to the brain telling it which tastes have been detected. Taste buds are most sensitive to bitter-tasting foods. This is really useful, because poisonous foods usually have a bitter taste – so

you know very quickly that you should spit them out. Your tongue can also tell if food is rough or smooth, hot or cold, or even painful (like chillies!).

All in flavour

Sometimes your senses work together. Flavour is actually a combination of taste and smell that enables you to identify different foods. When you catch a cold and can't smell properly because your nose is blocked up, food loses much of its flavour. This shows that flavour relies more on smell than it does on taste.

THIS CROSS-SECTION
THROUGH PAPILLAE
SHOWS THE TASTE
BUDS (THE LIGHT
BLOBS) ALONG
THEIR SIDES.

ALL EARS

From the whizz-bang of fireworks to the buzzing of a bee, the world around us is alive with sounds. We can hear these sounds thanks to the sense organs we call ears. Ears enable us to listen to our friends' jokes and enjoy our favourite music. But to some animals, the sense of hearing plays a more important role, helping them to find food and steer clear of hungry predators.

Look ear

A quick glance at your fellow humans (don't stare!) reveals that ears come in all shapes and sizes. But the flap on the side of the head that we refer to as an "ear" is just the visible part of a larger structure. The main part of the ear is buried and protected inside the skull. While the same is true of other mammals, from aardvarks to zebras, and of birds (although they don't have ear flaps), some animals detect sounds with different parts of their bodies. Spiders, for example, pick up sounds with the hairs on their legs, while earwigs use the pincers at the rear of their abdomen as hearing organs.

Sound waves

Wherever their "ears" might be, all animals use them to detect the same thing – sound waves. All that's needed to produce sound waves is something that causes the air to vibrate, such as a lion roaring, cymbals clashing, or a flash of lightning. The vibrations travel out from their source, rippling through the air

YOU CAN CLEARLY SEE THIS FROG'S HUGE EARDRUM, BECAUSE IT HAS NO EAR FLAP ON THE SIDE OF ITS HEAD.

as waves of high and low pressure.

If you're standing in the path of these sound waves, your ears will detect them. This is where the flaps on the side of the head come in handy. They funnel incoming sound waves along a tunnel in the skull called the ear canal. It contains a yellowy-brown wax that helps to keep your ears clean. The yucky wax also puts off insects that think your ears might make a cosy home.

Stretched across the inner end of the ear canal is a very thin sheet of skin called the eardrum. When sound waves hit it, the eardrum bounces in and out, vibrating just like the skin of a real drum.

WHEN A LION ROARS, ITS VOCAL CORDS VIBRATE AND SET UP STRONG SOUND WAVES IN THE AIR.

B ony link

Just behind the eardrum are three bones called the hammer, anvil, and stirrup. Together, they are known as the ossicles. They are the tiniest bones in the body, with the smallest, the stirrup, being no bigger than a grain of rice. The ossicles form a bony chain that links the eardrum to the inner ear.

When sounds hit the eardrum and make it vibrate, the ossicles rock back and forth, transmitting

THE PINK OVAL IN THIS MAGNIFIED IMAGE IS A HUMAN EARDRUM. THE BONE YOU CAN SEE TOUCHING THE EARDRUM IS THE HAMMER, ONE OF THE OSSICLES.

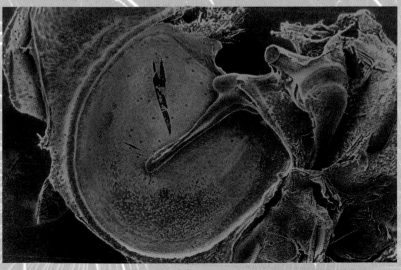

sound vibrations further into the ear. The tiny ossicles also amplify sounds – that is, make them louder.

Popping ears

Ever felt your ears "popping"? It happens when you're on a train that goes into a tunnel, or on a plane that is either taking off or landing. At first, you feel a little deaf, but if you yawn or suck a sweet – "pop!" – your hearing returns to normal.

The bony chamber in the skull that contains the ossicles is linked to the back of the throat by a tube that is usually closed. As a plane takes off, the air pressure in the cabin rapidly drops, so that it's much less than the pressure inside your ears. This pressure difference stops your eardrums and ossicles from vibrating properly, and you can't hear as well as usual. Sucking a sweet or yawning opens up the tubes to your throat. This allows air to move in or out of the middle part of your ears, equalizing the pressures inside and outside your head with a "pop".

Bending hairs

We have seen how sound waves make the eardrum vibrate and

the ossicles wobble. What next? Well, one of the wobbling ossicles – the stirrup – batters against the oval window, a kind of mini-eardrum that covers the opening to the inner ear.

The innermost part of your ear – a snail-shaped structure called the cochlea – is filled with liquid and contains about 15,000 sound sensors known as hair cells. On

the brain saying, "Listen up!"

The auditory (hearing) areas of the cerebral cortex, which are near to your temples, sort out the loudness, rhythm, and pitch (whether high or low) of the sounds. The nearby association areas then compare the sounds with ones you've experienced before, so you can tell a rock band from an opera singer.

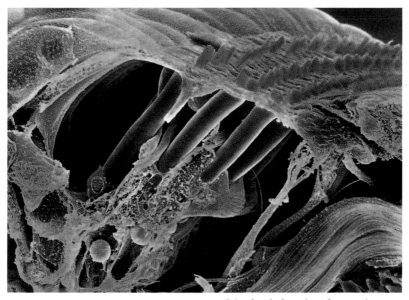

INSIDE THE SOUND-DETECTING COCHLEA, SENSORY HAIRS (ORANGE) PROJECT FROM THE TOP OF HAIR CELLS (RED).

the top of each cell are up to 100 hair-like projections. When the oval window vibrates as it's struck by the stirrup, ripples spread out through the fluid in the cochlea. These ripples bend the "hairs" and cause the hair cells to send nerve impulses to

It's the left side of your brain that deals with identifying and naming sounds, while the right side focuses on the quality of both sounds and music.

Which pitch?

From the squeakiness of a door hinge that needs oiling to the boom-boom of a bass drum on a CD track, everyday sounds

BATS HUNT
INSECTS BY SENDING
OUT PULSES OF HIGH-
PITCHED SOUND
THAT BOUNCE BACK
OFF THEIR PREY.

are close together and they
follow each other quickly, the
sound is high pitched. If the
waves are far apart and there
are fewer of them per second,
the sound will have a low pitch.

As we get older, we start to
lose the ability to hear the
high-pitched sounds
we could when we
were younger. But
some animals,
such as cats and
bats, can detect
ultrasounds –
sounds with a much
higher pitch than any human
can hear. Cats can hear the
ultrasound noises made
by mice and other prey.
The serval, a type of
African cat, listens out for
these high-pitched squeaks,
aided by large ear flaps that
pinpoint the direction the
sounds are coming from. Once
prey is in range, the serval leaps
and pounces on its prey,
squashing the poor victim
beneath its paws.

contain a vast range of different
pitches. A sound's pitch – or
frequency, as scientists call it –
depends on how close together
the sound waves are (in other
words, how many waves there
are per second). If the waves

Seeing with sound

When it comes to using
ultrasound, bats are even more
sophisticated. They send out
pulses of ultrasound that
bounce off both objects and

THE SERVAL HAS LARGE EAR FLAPS THAT
ENABLE IT TO LOCATE SMALL PREY IN LONG
GRASS BY SOUND ALONE.

prey, returning to the bat's big ears as echoes. The echoes give the bat a "sound picture" of its surroundings – something that's really useful for an animal that flies around at night! This is known as echolocation. It enables the bats to avoid bumping into trees and cliffs, and also to home in on juicy moths and other prey – even though they can't see them in the pitch dark.

Low pitch

It's not just high-pitched sounds that we can't hear. Baleen whales (the really big ones that feed on tiny plankton) produce very low-pitched sounds that travel hundreds of kilometres through the ocean. These infrasounds – the opposite of ultrasounds – allow whale groups to keep in touch over vast distances.

Back on land, elephants can make low-pitched growling noises that only other elephants can hear. Travelling through the air, the growls can be picked up by the ears of other elephants up to 10 km (6 miles) away. Recent research has found that these infrasounds travel even further through the ground of the African savanna (grassland) than through the air. Scientists

TO ATTRACT FEMALES, A MALE HUMPBACK WHALE SINGS A LONG, HAUNTING, LOW-PITCHED SONG FOR HOURS ON END.

A COCHLEAR IMPLANT USES A MICROPHONE ON THE HEAD TO SEND SIGNALS TO AN ELECTRONIC DEVICE INSIDE THE EAR.

believe that elephants detect the ground vibrations not with their ears, but with sensitive touch sensors in the tip of their trunk.

Decibel damage

If an elephant trumpeted in your ear, you'd certainly know about it. Contrast that noisy trumpeting with a whispered comment that you can barely hear. Those two extremes sum up the other characteristic of sounds – their loudness. How loud a sound is depends on the size of the sound waves. Loud sounds have big waves that create large ripples in the fluid of the cochlea.

Anyone who is exposed to loud sounds for long periods risks becoming deaf because they can damage the delicate hair cells in the cochlea. There are lots of causes of deafness, of course. In the past, the only hearing aids available were ear trumpets, which channelled extra sound into the ear, but they weren't very effective. Today's hearing aids use electronics to amplify sounds entering the ear. Some people have a tiny electronic device, called an implant, inserted into their cochlea. A microphone on the outside of the head picks up sounds and changes them into

FOR CENTURIES, EAR TRUMPETS WERE THE ONLY AIDS FOR PEOPLE WITH POOR HEARING.

electrical signals, which the implant passes on to the brain.

I n balance

The inner ear is home to more than just the cochlea. In other parts, called the semicircular canals and the vestibule, there are different types of hair cells. These sensors detect whether your body is upside down or the right way up, and whether it's moving forwards, backwards, or sideways. The brain combines the messages it receives from these sensors with those from your eyes, pressure sensors in your feet, and sensors in your muscles and joints. Together, they give the brain a picture of your body's position in space. This is your sense of balance.

Sometimes your sense of balance gets confused. Travelling by car, plane, or boat, you may feel that you're not really moving, because you are looking at a nearby object such as a book. However, sensors in the inner ear tell your brain that you really are in motion.

This can make some people feel sick, which is why airlines put sick-bags in front of you on planes to avoid an unpleasant mess! Here's a tip if you suffer from motion sickness – focus your eyes on the horizon.

LOG ON... discovery.com/flash/body/ http://yucky.kids.

TIGHTROPE WALKERS USE LONG POLES TO HELP THEM BALANCE AS THEY PERFORM THEIR DARE-DEVIL ANTICS.

LOOKING AT LIFE

Of all our senses, vision is certainly the most important. Our eyes are packed with sensors that, when hit by light from our surroundings, send electrical signals racing to the back of the brain. The signals are used by the brain to create detailed, full-colour, 3-D images of the outside world so that we can see. Most animals can see, but their eyes are not always the same as our own.

Simple eyes

To see some of the simplest eyes, take a look at flatworms. Most flatworms are aquatic, living in the sea or in freshwater. To avoid the attention of peckish predators, they spend their time in darkness under rocks or shells. They find these cosy hideaways using tiny eyespots at the front of their body. These eyespots don't allow flatworms to "see"

SIMPLE EYES

A FLATWORM'S SIMPLE EYES ENABLE IT TO STEER CLEAR OF BRIGHT LIGHT.

their surroundings, but they can detect the difference between light and dark. Shine a torch at a flatworm and it'll soon slide away into the darkness.

Many facets

For a more sophisticated type of eye, let's turn to the world of insects. Dragonflies, mantises, beetles, and many other insects have "compound eyes". These are the big, bulging things that occupy most of the insect's head. Look at a compound eye under a microscope, and you'll see that its surface is made up hundreds, or even thousands, of six-sided structures called facets. Under each facet is a tiny cylinder with a lens to focus light at the top

THIS IS A CLOSE-UP VIEW OF A HOVERFLY'S COMPOUND EYE. MANY INSECTS HAVE BOTH SIMPLE AND COMPOUND EYES.

and a sensor to detect light at the bottom. These cylinders collect light from the insect's surroundings. We don't know exactly what an insect can see with its compound eyes, but we do know that the image produced by its brain is not as clear as the one we see. What is clear is that compound eyes are incredibly good at spotting the slightest of movements – as you'll know if you've ever tried to swat a fly!

Prey spotters

Eagles and other birds of prey need to be able to see clearly over long distances to find and catch rabbits, mice, and other favourite foods. Their eyes are very much like ours, but their ability to see things in detail is up to eight times better.

BIRDS OF PREY, LIKE EAGLES, HAVE THE BEST EYESIGHT IN THE BIRD WORLD.

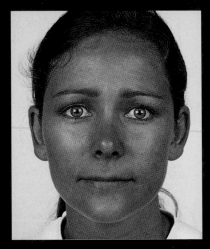

HUMAN EYES HAVE A WHITE PART TO MAKE THEM STAND OUT FROM THE FACE, WHEREAS A CHIMP'S DARK EYES DO NOT.

In fact, it's so good that a soaring golden eagle can spot a rabbit about 2 km (1.2 miles) away.

Front view

Eagles and other birds of prey have forward-facing eyes, which provide overlapping views that the brain uses to give a 3-D picture. This allows animals to judge distances accurately –

WEIRD WORLD

THE PATTERNS IN YOUR IRIS ARE UNIQUE TO YOU. IN THE FUTURE, IRIS SCANNERS WILL BE USED TO "READ" YOUR EYES AND PROVIDE A MEANS OF FRAUD-FREE PERSONAL IDENTIFICATION.

something that's essential for hunters that pounce on their prey. It's also crucial for tree-dwellers, like monkeys and apes, that leap from branch to branch.

Having the same ancestors as apes, we too have forward-facing eyes. But human eyes differ from those of chimpanzees, our closest ape relatives. We have a coloured iris (the bit around the black pupil) and a white sclera (the bit around the iris), whereas both a chimp's iris and sclera are brown. White scleras highlight our eyes so that we can use them to communicate – we look at each other's eyes as we talk. This contrasts with apes, whose eyes do not stand out from their face, which is useful when they're trying to hide from an enemy.

On track

Only a small part of the human eye is visible – the rest is tucked

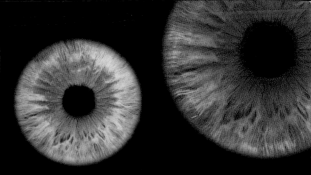

away in a protective cup in the skull called the orbit. The globe-shaped eye is mostly covered by the tough sclera. Six muscles pull on the sclera to move the eye up, down, left, and right. They let you scan the scene in front of you or track a speeding object without moving your head. The muscles also produce tiny jerky movements called saccades.

When you look at someone's face, you might think your eyes are focused on the person's nose, but they are actually moving non-stop as they scan the whole face. No matter how hard you try, you just can't stop your eyes making these saccades.

eye through the pupil – a dark hole surrounded by a muscular ring known as the iris. The colour of the iris depends on a brown pigment called melanin – the same stuff that colours the skin. If the iris contains lots of melanin, it will obviously be brown. But if there isn't very much melanin, then the iris can be green, grey, or blue.

The iris controls the pupil's size. In bright light, the pupil shrinks to prevent too much

Iris variety

At the front of the eye is a clear zone, called the cornea, that allows light to pass through. The light then enters the main part of the

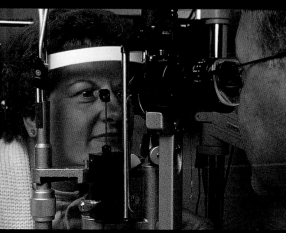

THIS OPTICIAN IS USING A SLIT LAMP TO EXAMINE A PATIENT'S EYES. HE MAY THEN PRESCRIBE GLASSES OR CONTACT LENSES.

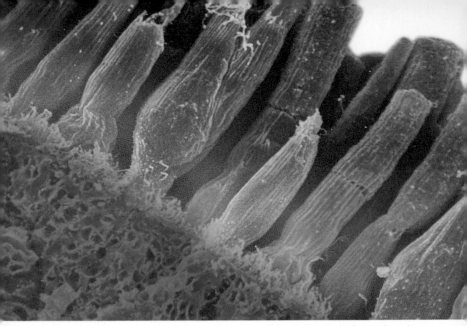

THE COLUMN-LIKE RODS (DARK BLUE) AND DUMPY CONES (LIGHT BLUE) ARE THE TWO TYPES OF SENSOR FOUND IN THE RETINA.

light from getting into the eye and damaging it. In dim light, the pupil enlarges to let in as much light as possible and help you see better.

Light sensors

Lining the inside of the back of the eye is a layer of sensors called the retina. There are two types of sensor, each named according to its shape. The most numerous are rods, which are found just about everywhere in the retina. They work best in dim light, and enable you to see things in black and white. Rods don't work very well in bright light, and take a bit of time to start working if you suddenly switch from bright to dim conditions – that's why it takes a while to get used to the dark if you go into a cinema when the lights are down. There are far fewer of the dumpy cone sensors. Most are concentrated in the central area of the retina, which is where light from objects directly in front of the eye falls. Cones work best in bright light. They let you see in colour, and view things in fine detail. Together, rods and cones make up more than 70 per cent of the body's sensors.

Missing colours

Daylight is made up of light of many different colours. There are three types of cone in the retina. They detect green, red, and blue light respectively.

When light hits the retina, the cones rattle off messages to the brain telling it the amount of red, green, and blue light that's coming from outside. The brain mixes these three primary colours, as they are known, to give every other colour and shade. That's how we can see a full-colour image of our surroundings. Some people, usually males, are "colour blind", which means that they lack one type of cone. In the most common form of colour blindness, people can't tell green and red apart.

A SHORT-SIGHTED WOMAN INSERTS A CONTACT LENS INTO HER EYE TO CORRECT HER VISION AND HELP HER SEE NORMALLY.

Blind spot

One place where there are no rods or cones is the blind spot. This is where the optic nerve, which carries impulses from rods and cones, leaves on its way to the brain. We don't notice the "gap" that the blind spot leaves in our vision, because the brain "fills in" the vacant area for us.

Out of focus

Of course, it's no good letting light fall on the retina unless it's in focus. The cornea, at the front of the eye, and the squashy lens just behind the pupil, focus light from an object to produce a clear, upside-down image on the retina. In some people, the lens, cornea, or eyeball is misshapen. This causes vision defects in which light is either focused in front of the retina (short sight) or behind it (long sight). Fortunately, eye problems

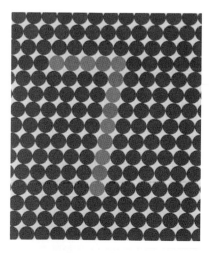

CHARTS LIKE THIS ARE USED TO TEST A PERSON FOR COLOUR BLINDNESS. PEOPLE WITH NORMAL VISION SEE THE NUMBER 7.

THIS CT SCAN "SLICES" ACROSS THE HEAD TO SHOW THE OPTIC NERVES THAT CARRY IMPULSES FROM THE EYES TO THE BRAIN.

like these can be corrected with glasses or contact lenses, which help to focus light in the correct place.

EYEBALL   OPTIC NERVE   VISUAL AREA OF THE BRAIN

S orting it all out

While the rods and cones in the eye detect light, the brain sorts out the stream of electrical impulses from these sensors so that we can actually see pictures of the outside world. The visual area of the cortex, at the back the brain, is divided into many different sections. Each one deals with a particular aspect of sight, such as colour, shape, movement, size, depth, and so on. All these elements

are then reassembled so that you "see" one complete picture.

B ee view

Some animals are able to see light that is invisible to human eyes. Insects, for example, can see ultraviolet light – the part of sunlight that can burn people's skin. So, when buzzing around in search of food, a bee's eyes can pick up the ultraviolet rays reflected off flower petals. This enables it to see the dark marks

HUMAN EYES SEE THIS FLOWER AS YELLOW, BUT A BEE'S ULTRAVIOLET VISION SHOWS IT AS BLUE WITH DARK MARKINGS.

on the petals – invisible to our own eyes – that guide insects to the nectar that they feed on.

Heat seeker

Pit vipers, such as rattlesnakes, are snakes with poor eyesight. But they do have special pit

light. They tend to have large eyes to let in plenty of light, and some, such as cats, have a reflective layer inside the eyes called the tapetum. It makes light bounce around inside the eye so that it gets detected more efficiently by the retina. You

AT NIGHT, A CAT'S VISION IS SIX TIMES BETTER THAN YOUR OWN

organs between their eyes and nostrils. These pick up infra-red (heat) radiation given off by warm-blooded prey such as juicy mice. The pit organs send nerve messages to the snake's brain, which produces a "heat picture" of its surroundings. This allows the snake to spot its prey, strike out, and sink its fangs accurately into the victim's furry body – even in the pitch-dark of night.

Night sight

It's not just snakes that hunt at night. Other animals, such as cats, owls, and bushbabies, can also search for food in the dark. These animals don't need pit organs, because their eyes work extremely well in poor

can see the tapetum in action when a cat gets caught in a car's headlights at night. The tapetum reflects the light, giving the cat's eyes an eerie glow.

TORCHLIGHT REFLECTS FROM THE TAPETUM IN A CAT'S EYES.

BRAIN TEASERS

Can you believe everything that you see? Of course not! We know that the amazing feats of magicians are just clever "tricks". But if our brains are so clever, why are we bamboozled by these deceptions? On the next few pages you'll find examples of how your brain can be fooled into seeing things the wrong way. And you'll also find out why this happens.

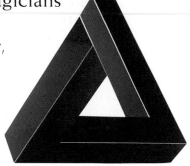

THE TRIBAR IS AN "IMPOSSIBLE" SHAPE. IT CAN BE DRAWN, BUT IT COULD NEVER EXIST AS AN OBJECT IN REAL LIFE.

What is that?

Every second, your brain is bombarded with nerve impulses from sensors in your eyes. The impulses are generated by the patterns that form on the retina as light reflects into your eyes from objects around you. To identify what's in front of you, your brain compares the patterns with those from previous visual experiences. If the information from your eyes is unclear, your brain has to guess what's being seen. Usually the brain guesses correctly, and the problem is solved – but not always.

Phantom triangle

Let's start our tour of brain teasers with the phantom triangle. Look at the picture on the left and you'll see two triangles. Now look at it again,

CAN YOU SEE THE PHANTOM TRIANGLE?

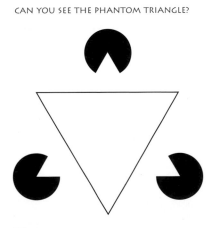

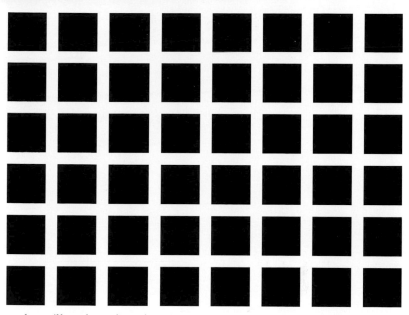

YOU SHOULD SEE SPOTS WHERE THE WHITE LINES CROSS ON HERMANN'S GRID.

and you'll realize that there's really only one triangle. Your brain assumes that the circles with the chunks cut out are part of a pattern. It "fills in" the lines between them, so that we think we can see a second triangle.

Although we're not aware of it, the brain is constantly filling blank spaces in our vision with lines and dots. Normally, this is helpful, as it gives us a complete view of our surroundings. But sometimes, as in this case, it produces an optical illusion.

S pots before the eyes

Sometimes the brain is fooled by the messages coming from the eyes. Take a look at the pattern of squares and lines at the top of this page, called a Hermann's grid. Where the lines cross you will see grey spots, even though there aren't any there. As light from a crossing point falls on the retina, the sensors receiving light from the middle of the cross shut down. But the sensors around them keep firing off

VENTRILOQUISTS TRICK THEIR AUDIENCE BY KEEPING THE HEAD AND MOUTH OF THE DUMMY MOVING AS A DISTRACTION.

messages to the brain. Your brain "sees" a spot (where the sensors aren't firing) surrounded by bright white lines (where they are firing).

Magic act

The ability of eye sensors to shut down is used by magicians. Think up a trick in which an object has to disappear. Make the thing that is going to vanish black, and then place it against a black background. Surround it with shiny metal rings or bars, or perhaps a brilliant white cloth. Just as with Hermann's grid, the bright light reflecting off the metal or cloth makes the central sensors (which would normally detect the black object) shut down. The black object seems to "disappear", and the audience is fooled by the magician.

What a dummy

Other stage performers who use visual tricks to confuse their audience are ventriloquists. These entertainers can speak without moving their lips,

LOG ON...
http://library.thinkquest.
org/J0110336/home.htm

"throwing" their voice so that it seems as though their dummy is actually talking.

However, there's far more to ventriloquism than throwing your voice. A ventriloquist's act also relies on well-timed dummy movements. When we see the dummy's mouth moving, our brain automatically assumes that the moving part is the source of the sound – and the dummy appears to talk. And

same length (you can test this with a ruler). It's the other lines – the context – that make the lines appear longer or shorter than they really are.

B end those lines

Context can also "bend" straight lines. In the fan illusion on page 74, the lines radiating out

MAGIC TRICKS WORK BY FOOLING THE VIEWER'S EYES AND BRAIN

while we watch the dummy, we don't focus on the mouth or throat of the ventriloquist, who is really making the sounds.

H ow long?

As you have seen, your brain uses both previous experience and the surroundings of an object to make sense (or not) of what the eyes are looking at. The surroundings, or "context", of an object can often be crucial to how you see the object.

Here's an example of how context affects what we see. Have a look at the two vertical lines on the right. Which do you think is the longer line? Well, in fact, they are both the

from the centre make the two vertical lines look curved. When you put a ruler beside them, it's obvious to the brain

WHICH LINE IS THE LONGER?

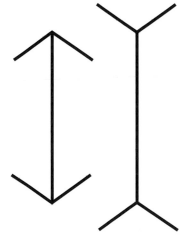

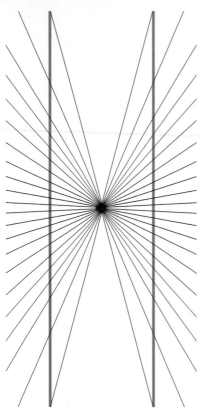

THE VERTICAL LINES IN THIS FAN ILLUSION ARE STRAIGHT, BUT THEY LOOK CURVED.

must decide whether the white or the black is the background (the context).

In depth

For hundreds of years, artists have used visual tricks to make their paintings more lifelike. When we look at objects, we see them in three dimensions – they have height, width, and depth. Artists use something called perspective to give a painting "depth" and make it more realistic. This tricks the brain into thinking that what it sees is three-dimensional (3-D), even though it's really a flat, two-dimensional (2-D) image. The artists make "distant" objects in the background –

that the lines really are straight. But take away the ruler, and trickery takes over once again.

Foreground or background?

Here's a puzzle in which the brain finds it difficult to separate an object from its context. Look at the picture on the right. You may see two faces on a white background, or a white vase on a black background. But your brain won't let you see both at the same time. Either the faces have to be in the foreground, or the vase does. Your brain

YOU MAY SEE A VASE OR A PAIR OF FACES... BUT YOU WON'T SEE BOTH AT ONCE.

THE 16TH-CENTURY ARTIST DE VRIES USED
PERSPECTIVE TO GIVE THIS PAINTING A
NATURAL FEELING OF DEPTH.

such as buildings, trees, or
people – smaller than "nearer"
ones in the foreground.

B lending in

Creating confusion between
foreground and background can
be really useful – and not just
to humans. Soldiers on patrol
paint green or brown stripes on
their faces so that they blend in
with the background vegetation.
The enemy cannot tell the
difference between foreground
(face) and background (trees).

THIS TIGER'S STRIPED COAT HELPS TO BREAK
UP ITS OUTLINE AND MAKE IT ALMOST
INVISIBLE IN LONG GRASS.

A tiger's stripes do the same as
the soldiers' face paint, enabling
the tiger to "disappear" in tall
grasses and hide from prey.
Using colours and patterns to
blend in with the surroundings
is called camouflage.

YOUR BRAIN CAN MAKE SENSE OF PARTS OF THIS PICTURE, BUT NOT THE WHOLE SCENE.

That's impossible!

While the brain can make sense of most things it sees, a few are just impossible for it to work out. These are "3-D" objects and scenes – like the tribar on page 70 and the picture above – that can be drawn, but which could never exist in real life. The brain uses things like relative size, movement, and the slightly different view it gets from each eye to build up a 3-D picture of the world. But in the case of "impossible" objects and images, the brain registers what the eyes are looking at, but it can't make total sense of it. Instead, the brain has to settle for understanding parts of the impossible image, and ignoring the "bigger picture".

Moving image

It's impossible for lines drawn on a piece of paper to move. Or is it? Focus on the circles below and they will appear to rotate. Your eyes scan the image with saccades (tiny, jerky movements), alternating rapidly between the black circles and the white spaces that separate them. The rod sensors in the retina (which can distinguish black and white) flash nerve signals on and off in response. Your brain interprets this rapid flashing as movement, and that's why the circles seem to rotate.

STARE AT THE CIRCLES TO SEE THEM MOVE!

Wrong colour

So much for movement – what about changing colours? Stare at the flag above for 30 seconds and then immediately look at a plain white piece of paper. You should see a ghostly image of the flag on the paper, with the flag appearing in its correct colours (red and white). As we saw in the last chapter, colour sensors in the retina called cones detect either red, green, or blue light. Specific cones may stop working if exposed to an object for a long time – such as when you stare at it – and other cones take over. That's why you see the flag in different "ghost" colours when you look away.

No interruption

Without another illusion, watching a TV programme or a movie at the cinema would be

COULD THIS FLAG EVER CHANGE COLOUR?

intensely irritating. TV and movie "pictures" are made up of a series of images that are flashed on the screen in quick succession. Your brain fuses all these images together, so that what you see is one continuous, moving performance. Luckily, your brain ignores the gaps between the images. If it didn't, you would be driven mad by the constant flickering!

WEIRD WORLD
IT'S MUCH MORE DIFFICULT TO RECOGNIZE FACES THAT ARE UPSIDE-DOWN, BECAUSE THE BRAIN'S FACE-RECOGNITION AREA TREATS THEM AS OBJECTS, NOT PARTS OF LIVING PEOPLE.

BEST BEHAVIOUR

When we're told to be on our best behaviour, we make sure that we don't do anything wrong. But there's much more to behaviour than just doing the right thing. From humans to horseflies, the behaviour of an animal is made up of all the things that it does, such as playing, feeding, resting, communicating with relatives, overcoming problems, and even chasing after mates.

It's instinctive

This topic of behaviour neatly brings together the activities of the brain and senses that we've explored in this book. Working together, the brain and senses enable you – and every other animal – to respond to the world around you. For example, when you hear someone call your name, your brain acts on the information coming in from your ears by sending a message to your muscles. You respond by turning towards the person calling out. Answering to your name is something that you learn as you grow up, but not all behaviour is learned.

Instinctive behaviour is built into the nervous system at birth. Many spiders spin silken webs to catch flies and other yummy insect snacks. But baby spiders don't have to figure out for themselves how to construct a web. They already have this knowledge when they hatch from their eggs, because they inherit their web-spinning skills from their parents.

A SPIDER INHERITS ITS ABILITY TO SPIN A WEB FROM ITS PARENTS.

IF A BABY IS PUT INTO WATER, ONE REFLEX
MAKES IT KICK AND PADDLE, WHILE
ANOTHER STOPS IT FROM BREATHING.

Reflex action

Also built into the nervous
system, so that they don't need
to be learned, are very simple
responses called reflexes. Each
reflex is a rapid reaction to a
particular stimulus that happens
automatically and always in the
same way. For example, when
food hits the back of your
throat (stimulus), you swallow
(reflex). Touch a sharp rose
thorn (stimulus), and you
immediately pull your hand
away (reflex). In the last case,
nerve impulses from pain
receptors in your finger go
straight through the spinal cord
to muscles in your arm, telling
the muscles to pull your hand
away. It's only a bit later that
nerve impulses reach your brain
and you feel the pain, shouting
"Ouch!" Other familiar reflexes
include shivering, sweating,
blushing, and sneezing.

Humans are born with some
reflexes that disappear within a
few months. If a small baby is
placed in a swimming pool, for
example, he or she will swim
underwater quite happily. A
reflex action, called the diving
reflex, closes off the entrance
to the lungs so the baby doesn't
swallow any water and drown.

WEIRD WORLD
A TREE-LIVING LIZARD CALLED A
CHAMELEON CHANGES COLOUR
TO MATCH ITS MOOD! NERVE
SIGNALS FROM THE BRAIN ALTER
A CHAMELEON'S SKIN TONES
ACCORDING TO WHETHER
IT'S ANGRY OR CONTENT.

ZOOLOGIST KONRAD LORENZ (1903–89) WAS THE FIRST THING THAT THESE GEESE SAW AFTER HATCHING, SO THEY FOLLOWED HIM ABOUT AS IF HE WERE THEIR MOTHER.

L earning how to behave

So much for built-in behaviour. How about a bit of learning? We've already seen, in an earlier chapter, how we pick up different types of behaviour during our lifetime, from learning to walk and talk to using a computer. And we're not the only animals to learn, either. For a really simple example of learning, look at the behaviour of baby ducks, or geese, just after they hatch. They rapidly learn to follow their mother everywhere, whether it's paddling across a pond or crossing a busy road. This rapid bonding – called imprinting – increases the ducklings' (or goslings') chances of survival. In fact, giving us a better chance of survival is the purpose of all types of behaviour, whether it's learned or "built in".

B rain play

Play is natural behaviour – not only for young humans, but also for many other young mammals. But what's the point of it? Why do children enjoy games, rough-and-tumble, and make-believe? Scientists think that play is an important part of growing up.

PLAY FIGHTING PREPARES THESE YOUNG BROWN BEARS FOR THE REAL FIGHTS THAT THEY'LL HAVE AS ADULTS.

CHIMPS CAN MAKE AND USE
SIMPLE TOOLS – IN THIS CASE, A
STICK FOR HOOKING TERMITES
OUT OF THEIR MOUNDS.

Play enables children to learn by experience all the skills they will need when they're older. Other young mammals, including lions, bears, and wolves, play too. Pretending to fight and pounce sharpens hunting skills. Play also teaches young animals how to behave inside a family group. Some scientists think that play is also vital for the brain to grow and develop properly.

A tool for the job

Another skill that we learn as children is how to use tools. At first, it involves simple tool skills, such as handling a spoon at mealtimes. As we get older, we move on to using computers, power drills, and other tools. We usually learn how to use tools from an adult. But once we've mastered the basics of a particular tool, we can use it for all sorts of tasks. This involves something called insight learning, which means being able to tackle new problems by reasoning and by drawing on past experiences.

The few other animal species that can use tools also learn their skills in a similar way. For example, by watching adults, a young chimpanzee finds out how to poke a stick into a nest to extract termites or ants. The angry insects cling tightly to the stick with their jaws, and get pulled out with it. The chimp slides the stick through its lips for a juicy, crunchy meal.

S ing that song

Of course, animals can't learn from each other without some form of communication. Whether by sound, gesture, scent, or other means, communication enables one animal to send a clear message to another that will alter its behaviour. The message may be a warning of approaching danger, an expression of aggression, a call to attract a lost youngster, or a host of other things.

Listen to birdsong, for example. Now, you may think that it's just a pretty background

CROSSING YOUR ARMS IS A SIGN THAT YOU ARE BEING DEFENSIVE

noise, but birds sing to tell other birds that a certain area is their territory – their "home" – in which they nest, feed, and bring up their young. They also sing to attract a mate.

BIRDS DON'T SING TO ENTERTAIN HUMANS, BUT TO DEFEND THEIR TERRITORY.

S poken word

We don't usually sing to our neighbours, but we do use sounds to communicate with each other in a way that other animals cannot. Humans use complex, spoken language.

In childhood, we first learn the basic elements of our own language, whether it's English, French, German, Arabic, or whatever. Then, as we get older, we rapidly improve our knowledge of words and our ability to use them. Some psychologists think that the framework for learning language is already present in our brains when we are born.

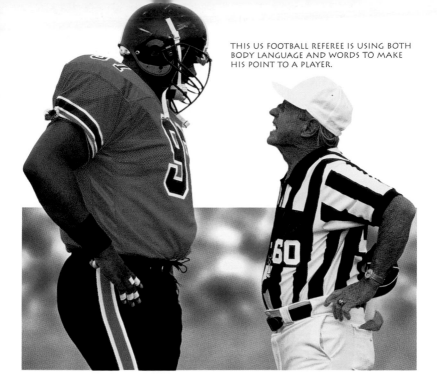

THIS US FOOTBALL REFEREE IS USING BOTH BODY LANGUAGE AND WORDS TO MAKE HIS POINT TO A PLAYER.

Body language

As well as spoken words, you can also communicate with your body. Your posture and the position of your arms and hands can indicate how you feel about the person you are talking to – often without you being aware of it. If you turn towards the other person and mirror their movements, for example, your "body language" shows that you like them.

One part of your body that shows clearly how you feel is your face. More than 30 tiny muscles tug on the skin of your face to express a wide range of feelings, including fear, sadness, happiness, anger, surprise, and disgust. These expressions are the same everywhere – a smile, for example, shows you're happy wherever you are in the world.

Getting aggressive

If communication doesn't have the desired effect, animals may resort to aggressive behaviour, especially when competing with other members of their species for food, space, or mates.

Male bighorn sheep in North America use their huge curved horns and armoured skulls to resolve disputes. Two males rush at each other head-on, and then bash their heads together with a loud bang. The winner of this headache-producing clash increases his status within the bighorn herd, and ends up with more mates.

Looking after others

It's often thought that every animal behaves selfishly, and that its sole concern is to ensure its survival. What's surprised ethologists (scientists who study animal behaviour) is that many social mammals – those that live in groups – show what is called altruistic behaviour. This means looking after fellow group members.

Meerkats are African mammals that show altruistic behaviour. Meerkats live in very organized social groups. While some group members hunt for spiders, scorpions, and other tasty morsels, others act as sentries. They scan the horizon for enemies, and call out a warning if they spot danger.

Other members of the meerkat group stay "at home"' to act as babysitters for young meerkats and protect them from predators. This behaviour may seem strange, but it makes sure that enough meerkats survive to breed and produce the next generation.

TWO MEERKATS KEEP A WATCH FOR ENEMIES WHILE OTHERS FEED NEARBY.

Good behaviour

We humans also show altruism whenever we behave unselfishly towards others. And we don't restrict this to our family and friends – many people spend their spare time doing voluntary work to help those in need.

Our large brains have made not only altruism but all sorts of other complex forms of behaviour possible. But as far as altruism is concerned, there's much more to it than making sure that the human race doesn't die out. Being considerate to others plays a vital part in holding societies together and helping to keep them peaceful.

REFERENCE SECTION

Whether you've finished reading *Brain*, or are turning to this section first, you'll find the information on the next eight pages really helpful. Here are all the historical facts and figures, background details, and unfamiliar words that will notch up your knowledge. You'll also find a list of website addresses – so, whether you want to surf the net or search out facts, these pages should turn you from an enthusiast into an expert.

BRAIN TIMELINE

c.500 BC
Greek physician and philosopher Alcmaeon of Croton proposes that the brain is the organ of thinking.

c.450 BC
Greek philosopher Plato states that the brain is the organ of intelligence, and that its spherical shape makes it the perfect home for reason.

c.350 BC
Greek philosopher Aristotle states that the heart, not the brain, is the organ of feeling and intelligence (a belief held long before by the ancient Egyptians).

c.280 BC
Herophilus of Alexandria revives the idea of the brain as the organ of thinking. He also describes the cerebrum and cerebellum, and discovers that nerves are channels of communication in the body.

c.160
Roman doctor Claudius Galen describes different types of nerve.

1268
English philosopher and scientist Roger Bacon records the use of spectacles to correct eye defects.

c.1500
Italian artist and scientist Leonardo da Vinci produces the first accurate drawings of the brain.

1543
Belgian doctor Andreas Vesalius publishes *The Structure of the Human Body*, which includes descriptions of the brain and nervous system.

1562
Italian anatomist Bartolomeo Eustachio describes the ear in detail in his book *The Examination of the Organ of Hearing*.

1662
French philosopher René Descartes' book *De Homine*, published 12 years after his death, puts forward ideas about the brain and mind, and describes reflexes.

1664
English doctor Thomas Willis describes the brain's blood supply.

1780
Italian doctor Luigi Galvani experiments with nerves, muscles, and electricity.

1792
Austrian doctor Franz Gall tries to find a link between behaviour and bumps on the skull. His research will form the basis of phrenology.

1801
French doctor Philippe Pinel suggests that mentally-ill people should be treated more humanely.

1811
Scottish anatomist Charles Bell describes nerve roots in the spine and shows that nerves consist of bundles of nerve cells.

1817
English doctor James Parkinson first describes a brain disorder that affects movement in some older people. It is now known as Parkinson's disease.

1837
Czech biologist Johannes Purkinje is the first to observe branching neurons (nerve cells) in the cerebellum.

1838
German scientist Theodor Schwann states that all living things are made

up of tiny units called cells.

1846

A hospital in Boston, USA, uses anaesthetic for the first time. Anaesthetics ensure that patients are unconscious and pain-free during an operation.

1848

American railroad worker Phineas Gage survives an explosion that forces an iron rod through the front of his brain. He suffers a behaviour change that indicates to scientists that the front part of the cerebrum controls personality.

1851

German physiologist Hermann von Helmholtz invents an instrument for looking inside the eye. It is called an ophthalmoscope.

1861

French doctor Pierre Paul Broca identifies the area (to be called Broca's area) on the left side of the brain that controls speech.

1872

Italian doctor Camillo Golgi devises a stain that for the first time shows the brain's nerve cells clearly under the microscope.

1874

Austrian doctor Karl Wernicke identifies the area (to be called Wernicke's area) on the left side of the brain that controls our understanding of language.

1875

Richard Caton, an English physiologist (a scientist who studies how the body works) discovers electrical activity in the brain.

1889

Spanish physiologist Ramón Santiago y Cajal states that the nervous system is made up of a network of distinct nerve cells (later called neurons) that do not touch.

1893

Death of French doctor Jean Martin Charcot, who discovered several nervous system diseases and laid the foundations for psychiatry.

1900

Austrian doctor Sigmund Freud publishes *The Interpretation of Dreams*, which contains the basic ideas of psychoanalysis.

1906

English physiologist Charles Sherrington publishes *The Integrative Action of the Nervous System*, an important book describing how the nervous system works.

1928

The electroencephalogram (EEG) is first used in medicine to record brain waves.

1952

British scientists Alan Hodgkin and Andrew Huxley describe the nature of nerve impulses.

1960s

Electron microscopes reveal the fine structure of neurons and confirm the existence of synapses.

1972

CT scanning is first used to produce images of body organs, including the brain and spinal cord.

1980s

MRI scanners are used to produce images of the inside of the brain.

2000

The first draft of the human genome project is completed. It identifies genes (the chemical instructions in our body) that affect the function and structure of the nervous system.

AMAZING FACTS

Brain and behaviour
• There are about 100 billion (100,000,000,000) nerve cells, or neurons, in the human brain.
• The brain also contains up to 5 trillion (5,000,000,000,000) "support cells" called glial cells.
• Many brain neurons last for a lifetime, but between the ages of 20 and 60 adults lose about 12,000 neurons every day that are never replaced.
• Some 250 million nerve fibres pass through the corpus callosum to link the two cerebral hemispheres.
• The brain is about 90 per cent water.
• A newborn human usually needs 16–20 hours sleep each day, a 5-year-old needs 10–11 hours, a 20-year-old 7–8 hours, and an 80-year-old just 5 hours.
• You can pull your hand away from a hot object in 0.03 seconds, because the spinal cord controls this reflex. If the nerve impulses had to go to your brain before you could act, it would take 0.8 seconds.

Nerves and neurons
• Stretched out, your nerves would extend more than 150,000 km (93,200 miles) – that's nearly four times the distance around the world.
• The widest nerve – the sciatic nerve that runs from the spinal cord into the leg – is 2 cm (0.8 in) wide.
• Nerves are made up of bundles containing thousands of neurons.
• A neuron can transmit 1,000 nerve impulses every second.
• Neurons include the longest cells in the body, up to 1 m (3.3 ft) in length. The shortest neurons are 1 mm (0.04 in) long.
• Humans are born with all the neurons they will ever have.

Senses
• Young people can hear sounds of a higher pitch than older people.
• Young people have about 10,000 taste buds, cats about 470, chickens 25, and pigs about 15,000. The number of human taste buds decreases with age.
• The nose can detect just one molecule of mercaptan (the incredibly smelly substance that skunks produce) diluted in 30 billion molecules of air.
• Taste bud cells are replaced after a week, while smell sensors last for a month.
• Humans can detect more than 10,000 smells but just four tastes.
• The eyes contain 70 per cent of the body's sensors. Each eye has about 125 million rods and 7 million cones.
• The eyes can detect about 10 million colours.
• Colour blindness affects about 1 in 12 males and 1 in 100 females. About 1 in 100,000 people can only see in black, white, and grey.
• At night, the eyes can detect a lighted candle 1.6 km (1 mile) away.

BRANCHES OF BRAIN MEDICINE

Electroencephalography
The use of electroencephalograms (EEGs), which record electrical activity in the brain as wavy lines (brain waves) on a graph or a screen.

Neurology
The branch of medicine that deals with the nervous system.

Neuropathology
The branch of medicine that deals with the causes and effects of diseases of the nervous system.

Neurophysiology
The study of how the nervous system works.

Neuropsychiatry
The branch of medicine that deals with the links between mental illness and damage to the nervous system.

Neurosurgery
Surgical treatment of disorders of the brain, spinal cord, and nerves.

Ophthalmology
The branch of medicine that deals with the eye and its diseases.

Otorhinolaryngology
The branch of medicine that deals with the ear, nose, and throat, and their diseases (often known as ENT).

Psychiatry
The branch of medicine that deals with mental illnesses and their treatment.

Psychoanalysis
The identification and treatment of mental disorders using a form of therapy that's based on the teachings of Sigmund Freud (1856–1939).

Psychology
The study of the brain and behaviour.

Psychopathology
The branch of psychiatry and psychology that deals with the diagnosis of abnormal mental processes.

Psychopharmacology
The study of the effects of drugs on the brain and behaviour.

Psychosurgery
The use of brain surgery to treat mental illness and alter behaviour.

Psychotherapy
The treatment of mental problems whereby a patient talks about his/her problems with a trained therapist.

PHOBIAS

Ablutophobia Fear of washing
Acrophobia Fear of heights
Agyrophobia Fear of crossing the street
Ailurophobia Fear of cats
Alliumophobia Fear of garlic
Arachibutyrophobia Fear of peanut butter sticking to the roof of the mouth
Aviophobia Fear of flying
Blennophobia Fear of slime
Bufonophobia Fear of toads
Claustrophobia Fear of very confined spaces

Coulrophobia Fear of clowns
Didaskaleinophobia Fear of going to school
Enetophobia Fear of pins
Ergophobia Fear of work
Frigophobia Fear of cold things
Isopterophobia Fear of termites
Koniophobia Fear of dust
Lachanophobia Fear of vegetables
Lilapsophobia Fear of tornadoes and hurricanes
Metrophobia Fear of poetry
Mycophobia Fear of mushrooms
Neophobia Fear of anything new
Nosocomephobia Fear of hospitals
Ophidiophobia Fear of snakes
Papyrophobia Fear of paper
Phobophobia Fear of phobias
Pogonophobia Fear of beards

Rhytiphobia Fear of getting wrinkles
Samhainophobia Fear of Halloween
Selachophobia Fear of sharks
Siderophobia Fear of stars
Tachophobia Fear of speed
Thalassophobia Fear of the sea
Uranophobia Fear of heaven
Venustraphobia Fear of beautiful women
Wiccaphobia Fear of witches and witchcraft
Xanthophobia Fear of the colour yellow
Xenophobia Fear of strangers or foreigners
Zemmiphobia Fear of the great mole rat

BRAIN WEBSITES

http://faculty.washington.edu/chudler/neurok.html
Neuroscience for kids, with a wide range of resources and links.
www.bbc.co.uk/health/kids/mind.shtml
Mind matters gives you helpful hints on how to cope with worry.
www.bbc.co.uk/science/humanbody/
About the human body including brain, nervous system, eyes, and ears.
www.brainpop.com/health/
An excellent kids' website on the human body and health, including the brain, nervous system, and senses. It includes quizzes, facts, and movies.
http://tqjunior.thinkquest.org/4371/
A wide range of resources about the brain and nervous system.
http://hhmi.org/senses/
An in-depth site devoted to seeing, hearing, and smelling the world.
www.illusionworks.com/
Demonstrations, explanations, and projects on optical and sensory illusions.
http://biology.about.com/cs/humanbrain1/
An advanced site that gives you the low-down on the different brain parts.
www9.biostr.washington.edu/da.html
An interactive brain atlas, with 3-D images of brain structures.

GLOSSARY

Antennae
The "feelers" of crustaceans and insects that detect touch and smell.

Association neuron
A neuron that relays signals between other neurons, and also processes information.

Axon
A neuron's long "tail" that carries nerve impulses away from the cell body. Also called a nerve fibre.

Blind spot
The part of the eye's retina where the optic nerve leaves the eye, and where light cannot be detected.

Brain
The part of an animal that receives information from sensors, and sends out signals to control the animal's behaviour and its body's activities.

Brain stem
The part of the brain that links it to the spinal cord, and which controls breathing and heart rate.

Carrion
The dead body of any animal.

Cell body
Part of neuron that contains the nerve cell's nucleus (control centre).

Cells
Tiny living units that are the basic building blocks of all living things.

Central nervous system (CNS)
The part of the nervous system that consists of the brain and spinal cord.

Cerebellum
The part of the brain that controls balance. It ensures that movements are smooth and co-ordinated.

Cerebral cortex
The thin outer layer of the cerebrum that processes information relating to thought and memory, senses such as seeing, and movement.

Cerebral hemisphere
One of the two halves – left and right – of the cerebrum.

Cerebrum
The largest part of the brain, which enables people to think and feel. It also controls body movements.

Cochlea
The coiled structure inside the ear that detects sounds.

Compound eye
An eye, found in crustaceans and insects, that is made up of many separate units, each containing a lens.

Consciousness
An awareness of one's self, surroundings, and existence.

Cones
One of two types of light sensor in the eye's retina, cones work in bright light and provide colour vision.

Cornea
The clear layer at the front of the eye that allows light in. The cornea helps to focus the light on the retina.

Corpus callosum
A band of nerve fibres that connects the left and right cerebral hemispheres.

Cranium
The part of the skull that surrounds the brain.

CT scan
A special type of X-ray that produces images of "slices" through the body.

Dendrite
The short filaments that carry nerve impulses to the cell body of a neuron.

Eardrum
The thin membrane at the end of the ear canal that vibrates when sound waves reach the ear.

Electroencephalogram (EEG)
A recording of brain waves produced by electrical activity in the brain.

Electron microscope
A powerful microscope that shows body cells and tissues in great detail.

Follicle
A pit deep in the skin from which hairs grow.

Glial cells
Nerve cells that support, feed, and protect neurons.

Imprinting
Behaviour found in some very young animals that memorize and follow their parents.

Infrasounds
Low-pitched sounds that cannot be heard by humans.

Instinct
A type of built-in behaviour that is inherited from parents.

Iris
The coloured part of the eye that alters the size of the pupil to change the amount of light entering the eye.

Jacobson's organ
A sense organ in the roof of the mouth of snakes and lizards that detects smells.

Limbic system
The part of the brain that controls our emotions.

Melanin
The brown pigment that colours the iris in the eye, as well as skin and hair.

Migraine
A severe headache that may be accompanied by disturbed vision and/or nausea.

Migration
An annual journey made by some animals to breed and/or find food.

Motor neuron
A neuron that carries nerve impulses away from the CNS to the muscles.

MRI scanner
A machine that uses magnetism and radiowaves to produce images of the inside of the body.

Mucus
A thick, slippery liquid that lines the respiratory (breathing) and digestive systems.

Myelin sheath
The fatty covering that protects and insulates the axon (nerve fibre) of some neurons.

Nerve
A cable-like bundle of neurons that links all body parts to the brain and the spinal cord.

Nerve fibre
Another name for an axon.

Nerve impulse
A tiny electrical signal that passes at high speed along a neuron.

Nerve net
A simple network of nerve cells (without a brain) found in anemones, jellyfish, and their relatives.

Nervous system
A system of interconnected neurons that collects information from the body, and sends out instructions to control it. Unlike a nerve net, a nervous system includes a brain.

Neurons
Nerve cells that make up the brain, spinal cord, and nerves. Neurons carry electrical signals at high speed.

Ossicles
Three tiny bones that carry vibrations from the eardrum to the inner ear.

Papillae
Tiny bumps on the the tongue.

PET scanner
A machine that uses radioactive chemicals to reveal activity inside the body.

Phantom pain
When people who have had a limb removed experience pain in their missing limb.

Pheromones
A chemical released by an animal that affects the behaviour of another animal of the same species.

Phobia
An irrational fear of a particular object, person, situation, or place.

Phrenology
A discredited belief that personality could be investigated by feeling the bumps on someone's head.

Pit organs
A pit viper's heat-detecting organs.

Pupil
The opening in the centre of the iris through which light enters the eye.

Receptor
Another name for a sensor.

Reflex
An automatic action, such as blinking, swallowing, or pulling the hand away from a sharp object.

Retina
The lining inside the eyeball that is packed with light sensors.

Rods
One of two types of light sensor in the retina. Rods work in dim light and provide black-and-white vision.

Saccades
Tiny, jerky eye movements that scan the view in front of the body.

Saliva
A watery liquid released into the mouth by the salivary glands, especially during chewing.

Sclera
The eye's tough, white outer layer.

Semicircular canals
Fluid-filled structures in the inner part of the ear that detect movement and help maintain balance.

Sensor
A cell or group of cells that can detect stimuli. Also called a receptor.

Sensory neuron
A neuron that carries nerve impulses from sensors to the CNS.

Spinal cord
A column of nervous tissue that relays messages between brain and body.

Stain
A dye used to colour cells so they can be seen under the microscope.

Stimulus (plural stimuli)
A change in the body's surroundings detected by a sensor that triggers a nerve impulse in a neuron.

Synaesthesia
The ability to mix senses, such as hearing colours or seeing sounds.

Synapse
The junction between two neurons, where they come extremely close to each other but do not quite touch.

Taste buds
Taste sensors located in the papillae.

Trepanning
The ancient practice of cutting holes in the skull to relieve pressure and allow "evil spirits" to escape.

Ultrasounds
High-pitched sounds that cannot be heard by humans.

Vertebrate
An animal with a backbone.

Zoologist
A scientist who studies animals.

INDEX

CREDITS

Dorling Kindersley would like to thank:

Marcus James for initial design concept, Dean Price for jacket design, and Chris Bernstein for the index.

Richard Walker would like to thank: Fran Jones, Stefan Podhorodecki, Steve Setford, Peter Radcliffe, and the rest of the team responsible for this book.

Illustrations by:

Peter Visscher 20–21b and Dave Hopkins 29t.

Additional photography by:

Geoff Brightling, Frank Greenaway, Dave King, Ranald Mckechnie, Susanna Price, Jules Selmes, Debi Treloar, Peter Visscher, David Ward, Jerry Young.

Picture Credits

The publisher would like to thank the following for their kind permission to reproduce their photographs:
a=above; c=centre; b=bottom; l=left; r=right; t=top

AKG London: 14; Erich Lessing 75t; M. C. Escher's "Relativity" c. 2001 Cordon Art B. V. – Baarn – Holland. All rights reserved 76tl.
British Museum: 13.
Bruce Coleman Ltd: 51; Franco Banfi 59; Jane Burton 69; John Cancalosi 63bl; Johnny Johnson 80b; Kim Taylor 52; Gunter Ziesler 75br.
Corbis: 60bl; Duomo 35b; Laura Dwight 34, 90–91; Owen Franken 35tr; Robbie Jack 72; Roger Ressmeyer 36b; Vince Streano 29br.
Robert Harding Picture Library: 79.
Courtesy of Honda Motor Company: 32.
The Image Bank: Jeff Hunter 54–55 background, 85; Terje Rakke 44.
Kobal Collection: 31.
Chris Mattison Nature Photographics: 4, 10.
N.H.P.A.: Agence Nature 11; Daryl Balfour 28; Laurie Campbell 82; Stephen Dalton 58tl, 78; Nigel J Dennis 84br; Martin Harvey 58bl, 64tr; Daniel Heuclin 50tr; Steve Robinson 81.
Oxford Scientific Films: Ralph Reinhold 46bl.

Pictor International: 42tl, 43, 48, 56, 61, 83.
Scala Group S.p.A.: Musei Capitolini Roma 33b.
Science Photo Library: 16, 25tl, 80tl; John Bavosi 30; Juergen Berger, Max-Planck Institute 18; Dr. G. Oran Bredberg 57; Mark Burnett 67bl; Scott Camazine 27bl; BSIP Chassenet 67tr; Suzanne L. & Joseph T. Collins 22b; CNRI 3, 15; Eye of Science 9; Don Fawcett 22t; GJLP-CNRI 1, 12bl, 86–87; Pascal Goetgheluck 38bl; John Greim 65br; Astrid & Hanns-Frieder 53; Adam Hart-Davis 5, 24; Jerrican 37tr; James King-Holmes 60tr; Mehau Kulyk 68t; S.R.Maglione 46t; Professor P. Motta & D. Palermo 23; Claude Nuridsany and Marie Perennou 68bl, 68br; Omikron 66; David Parker 65tl, 65tc, 65tr; Quest 6, 21t, 41, 55b; John Reader 12tr; J.C Revy 16–17 background; David Scharf 45, 63tr; Secchi-Lecaque/Roussel-Oclaf/CNRI 49; Geoff Tompkinson 26, 88–89; U.S. National Library of Medicine 39; M. I. Walker 62; Wellcome Dept of Cognitive Neurology 27cr; Andrew G. Wood 7, 47c; Kent Wood 40.

Book Jacket Credits

Front cover:
Science Photo Library: Geoff Tompkinson.
Back cover:
Science Photo Library: Adam Hart-Davis tr.

All other images © Dorling Kindersley.
For further information see:
www.dkimages.com